The

LEADERSHIP
DECISION

DECIDE TO LEAD TODAY

Dr. Catherine M. Rymsha

ISBN (paperback) 978-1-7357313-0-8
ISBN (ebook) 978-1-7357313-1-5
ISBN (audiobook) 978-1-7357313-2-2

Cover and interior design by MiblArt.
Editorial services by Sandra Wendel, Write On, Inc.

Published by The Leadership Decision
Contact the author at www.TheLeadershipDecision.com.

Contents

Introduction: We Are All Capable of Leadership

I've never heard a high school senior approaching their first year of college answer "leadership" when asked what they plan to study. Have you? Instead, they answer, "Management."

Management tends to go past the lips and into the ears instead. We all know people who have management degrees. You may have management degrees. People know what management is, or so they think. The listener will nod and say how wonderful it is that the young student wants to be in a management role, even remarking, "What a smart decision."

If this blossoming academic were to say "leadership" in answering that question, the inquirer might look puzzled. Unlike management, it's unfamiliar. How can anyone study leadership? What would that even entail? They don't know anyone with a leadership degree nor have one themselves. The idea seems crazy. Or does it?

Management is learned. It's clean. Easily defined in job descriptions aligned with a specific placement within a hierarchy of a corporation. Leadership is experienced. It's messy. Gray. Open to interpretation with fewer formal boundaries saying what you can do and what you can't. Management ties the humanness of leadership in a different box with a neatly wrapped bow that makes it more palatable. Yet, leadership is becoming the gift we prefer and also want to give.

Discussions in the business world, in the news, in classrooms, and over cocktails are changing and moving from concepts of management to that of the importance of leadership. We can't escape leadership these days with its presence in LinkedIn posts, in the news, and with internal corporate-driven leadership development programs. We hear about leadership all the time.

But why? Why does studying and understanding leadership matter now more than it did twenty years ago? And why is this area still growing in popularity even though leadership is far from being a new topic or idea compared to many others? Why are we even talking about this or reading a book about it? Why do we want to be leaders? Honestly, it's hard to say.

Is it because of the internet and increased awareness? Sure. Is it because of the changing workforce with baby boomers, millennials, and the like? Could be. Is it possibly due to one of many blanketed business words and terms? Globalization? Competitive advantage? Work/life integration? Maybe.

Alternatively, is it because people realize that studying leadership, understanding leadership, and being a leader is a more holistic and comprehensive way to work with people and to ensure organizational as well as life success?

Yes.

We are aware of leadership now more than ever. We talk about it more. We read about it more. We all need and want more leaders in our worlds and in our lives ranging from those we work with each day to those we see holding political leadership positions to those we see leading within our communities. Plus, we're starved for good leaders and strong leadership. From that hunger, we want to be leaders in our own lives for our reasons too.

It doesn't matter why leadership has grown in popularity. What matters, though, is that we have leadership on the brain. We're leadership obsessed. We want to work for companies with strong leadership. We want our managers to be leaders (not just the boss). We want to be leaders. We see the need for leaders everywhere.

Regardless of why leadership is so important are the decisions we can make now to lead for ourselves, for those we love, for our communities, and for our work. And how we can take action to lead when we see an opportunity and make the decision to seize that opportunity and take initiative. Leadership and being a leader is as simple, and as complicated, as that. No matter where you are with your own understanding of leadership and its importance, by picking up this book, you are making the first decision to become a leader yourself. Congratulations.

About This Book

This book is focused on the A/P/E Model, which is a continuous cycle for you to make decisions about yourself as a leader in improving your ability and influence. This book varies from other leadership texts that focus specifically on skills and not on the process of actionable development. **A/P/E stands for awareness, practice, and evaluation.** The A/P/E Model serves as a guide on how we can make active decisions about our leadership ability, development, and growth.

In aligning to the A/P/E Model, Part I focuses on our awareness of leadership. This includes defining what leadership is, what it isn't, and why we may need to readdress how we view and define it both for ourselves and how we determine the value and the impact of those who lead. Is leadership simply a title at work? No. It's more. In realizing this, how can we create our own Leadership Brand based on how people perceive our leadership? I then look at another foundational element that I call the Leadership Lifestyle in how we lead and live.

Part II, the awareness section, addresses the A/P/E Model in further detail and explains how you can use it to take initiative. In reading, you will gain insight about how you can frame your decisions by using the A/P/E Model to enhance your leadership practice while also addressing practical solutions on how you can use this text in your life to make a difference that will matter to you.

The section on practice also introduces another framework called TOLL. TOLL is an acronym for timing, opportunity, looks, and likes, and this section discusses why each matters to us as leaders and to understanding, defining, and making our leadership decisions. Why TOLL? Because this introduces a level of reality that other books don't. In giving thought to TOLL, you can identify in your realities why things may not be changing in your life and career and how using this awareness framework, along with the A/P/E Model, can further aid in your decision-making and progress.

Part III illuminates commonly thought of attributes, skills, and behaviors that we evaluate and judge in people whom we consider leaders. This section aims to provide you with specific areas of focus to start your leadership decision-making journey. While one chapter addresses practical ways you can evaluate yourself with the A/P/E Model, another chapter gives you specific areas of practice.

Once you've defined and evaluated leadership to broaden your awareness, learned more about the A/P/E Model and how you can use this in your practice along with giving further consideration to the skills that will elevate you to leadership status, this discussion leads us to the fourth section. Part IV concludes with insight on uniting the concepts. In reading, you will find ways to think about your leadership: where you are, where you want to be, and how to feel empowered knowing that you can get there through your decisions.

As you read, you'll have a clearer understanding of the areas in your life that you can improve being a leader, ways you can further enhance your skills, and where, if anywhere, you need to make decisions and changes to further enhance your practice. You'll have the tools and understanding to make the decision to lead.

A Note on Anonymity

Becoming and being a leader can be viewed either as a collaborative effort in thinking about working with others, asking for feedback and coaching, and sharing best practices and results in a conversation, or it can be viewed as a private practice. Some may want to keep the practice of leadership to themselves for various reasons. One that I often hear is people being scared of being judged and hearing feedback that their practice isn't paying off. You can have reasons due to personal and work circumstances too. Alternatively, maybe some people don't feel fully supported and confident enough to share. Or they don't feel worthy of leadership.

Whatever the case may be, it may take time for some of us to be comfortable talking about our leadership with others, and that's okay. It can be hard at first to get comfortable saying, "I am a leader," or "I'm working on being a leader." Neither statement shows weakness or failure. It shows that you are trying and that you are aware. We are all capable of being leaders in whatever way that looks like to us.

You may want to start your practice as private and over time build up to soliciting feedback from others and sharing your practice and decision to lead. And that's okay. In keeping with the need for privacy within your leadership journey, and in relation to this particular book, I discuss situations and experiences that are unique to me from what I have studied and observed in others. I share these for the sake of helping you to think about your life, practice, and experiences to aid in your leadership decisions.

For those leaders who are not painted within the best of light, I have masked their identities. Maybe at the time or how they viewed particular circumstances, they thought their decisions were the right ones for whatever reason. Keep this in mind as we've all worked with and for people who made mistakes and who may have treated us or others poorly. The stories I use are from my own experiences at a variety of employers and from other stories that were shared with me through friends, peers, and family.

For those who aren't portrayed in the best of circumstances, maybe their behavior was on purpose or perhaps it was a mistake. Let's assume, for the most part, that their decisions were a mistake, so it doesn't dampen our journey and thoughts on leadership. We don't have to be, or even become, those people. We can't hold grudges for lousy leadership. However, we can learn from their mistakes. We can learn a lot from seeing bad behavior, experiencing bad leadership, and having people treat us in a way that we would never treat others. That, within itself, can be the most significant learning tool of all in helping us make better decisions about our leadership.

Why Are We Here?

If you're like me, you think about leadership. So maybe you're like me in that you ask yourself, "What makes a leader, a leader?" In trying to find the answer, I wanted to write a book that challenged the way people think about leadership.

Leadership was never meant to be part of my path. It was never a topic I considered or thought about. Growing up, I wanted to write. I went to college for English/communications with a focus on journalism and public relations at the Massachusetts College of Liberal Arts in North Adams, Massachusetts. When I graduated, I immediately looked into a master's degree to pursue my love of writing. I applied to a corporate communications program at Northeastern University in Boston. A few weeks after I applied, an admissions representative called to tell me that the program wouldn't be running due to low enrollment.

My heart sank. But she paused and what she said next would change my life. They were offering a program in leadership and many of the courses were similar. Anxious to complete my degree, I agreed to take the leadership program and found myself challenged in trying to figure out what makes a leader, a leader. After I completed my degree, I wanted to learn more and began my doctorate at Northeastern to further my understanding.

While I've studied leadership, I've experienced it, too, with both the good and the bad. I'm not an academic who sat on the sidelines observing and researching others. I spent over ten years in marketing/communications roles traveling the world to organize and market healthcare conferences that brought global leaders together to discuss the most pressing issues. I wrote speeches and traveled to educate people globally on payment card security. I began teaching during my marketing career while working full-time and pursuing my degrees.

I led learning and development within human resources for a software company where I helped develop leaders at all levels to be more effective. I worked my whole life at both the family farm on my mother's side picking beans, Brown Spring Farm in West Newbury, Massachusetts, and washing dishes at the luncheonette on my father's side, Taffy's in Newburyport, Massachusetts.

I've been told by leaders that I'm not good enough for leadership or for promotions. I've been told by some leaders that I'm everything they've always wanted in an employee. I've struggled at points in my career and in my life in wanting more and not knowing where to start, but turned to my parents who in those moments told me to "make the right decisions," and their advice always got me through it in trusting myself and what I was deciding.

From all of these experiences, I gained the insight, experience, and ambition to write this book that would challenge you to think realistically about your own decisions and how they were impacting your life and leadership.

After reading book after book, taking class after class, and listening to podcast after podcast about leadership myself, I struggled with the confusing messaging. Some positioned the concept of leadership in ways that made it seem almost unattainable, while others painted leadership in ways that seemed oversimplistic.

Leadership is just a skill, they would tell us, or just a promotion. Some of these people seemed out of touch in thinking about today's work environment in books written by people who may not have worked in the corporate setting for years, if ever, due to being buried deep in research about behavior and best practices within the halls of academia.

While I respect and see the value in what people have outlined in understanding leadership, the rest of us—

regardless of the title that we hold within a corporation or job or wherever we want to lead in life—need to know that leadership is possible. That's what makes this book different from others that focus on the skills only, not the action and initiative people need to take to truly lead.

Everyone and anyone can be a leader. Leadership isn't only for the selected few. Some disagree and think that leadership ability is something you're born with—or not. Some make the idea of leadership overly complicated. Some people think that taking certain classes or reading certain books or mixing the two is the only real preparation. We are all capable of leadership in what that looks like to us and in our own lives.

The reality is that leadership shouldn't be hidden away for only the brightest and best. Leadership is something that we are all capable of, and it can look different for everyone. It shouldn't be based on a score or ranking we get on some personality profile or behavioral analysis. We all can develop, change, and be leaders if we want it.

If you wake up and think, "Crap, I have to wake up, go to work, sit there all day, and act as [insert whatever your title is here] and then come home, parent, and somehow make a difference in the community or the world," this book is for you. This book is also for those of you who sometimes need a reminder about how you can take action from within the trap of mediocrity directly through your decisions.

Sometimes we wait around for things to happen to us. Promotions are given to justify our ability to lead. None of that matters. What matters is that you are making decisions about your leadership ability today. You are taking ownership in trying to live a Leadership Lifestyle within the A/P/E Model in gaining awareness (A) by taking action and initiative to practice (P) and then looking to those you trust, to those you lead, and to yourself for evaluation (E). Within the leadership decision framework, the A/P/E Model, you can begin to make changes to your leadership ability and your life.

Challenge yourself and think: Will you decide to lead today?

PART I:
Understanding Leadership

"I am not a product of my circumstances.
I am a product of my decisions."

Stephen Covey

1

Leadership Definition and Value

Describe a leader. Grab a pen and piece of paper or your phone and brainstorm for a minute or two. What words, phrases, or actions come to mind? Jot those down and keep that list close as you continue to read.

Maybe words like *strategic, collaborative, innovative, personable, confident,* and *successful* float to mind. Phrases stringing those words together may follow. Names of corporate leaders like a president or chief executive officer (CEO) of a leading company may fill your notepad.

Alternatively, even the CEO, vice president (VP), or people managers at the company where you work. Or politicians both national and local may come to mind. You may even think of a member of the community who leads initiatives and projects that you see make a difference, like fundraisers or cultural events. Or maybe a friend of yours who you think leads by example in the way they live their life.

Did you think of yourself? Do you define yourself as a leader in the way that you work, live your life, and make your decisions? If you happen to think about CEOs, VPs, or people managers, keep in mind that those are people in particular roles completing particular tasks and duties within a company. But does that equate to leadership? Maybe, but maybe not. We've all made mistakes in how we've defined leadership. How, you may ask?

We've romanticized leadership. We've taken it to dinner, been wowed by its overhyped and adjective-filled stories and profiles. We've even taken it to post-movie coffee and been blown away at the research, theory, behavioral analysis, and assessments that have helped leadership get to where it is today—high profile, sexy, and, somewhat, unattainable.

Let's face it: leadership is out of our league. How can one person be and do so much? Moreover, how can we expect that both from others and ourselves? We're not worthy of it, especially if we're not leading people formally in our role at work.

We define and understand leadership based on characteristics, behaviors, and traits that we associate with leaders. After all, it's a title! Many think we can't be leaders without a title. But we can. I can. You can. We've gone wrong in defining leadership and how we define people as leaders. Everyone's leadership definition is different. Everyone's idea of leadership is different. That's what makes thinking and talking about leadership so fascinating.

We sometimes may define leaders the way that we envision our future or desired selves. In thinking about ourselves, why do we want to be leaders based on our definitions and what we jotted down? Why do we buy books, listen to podcasts, attend lectures, and spend billions of dollars on this topic? We all have our reasons that we admire leadership or want to lead.

Maybe we see leadership aligning with power, and the idea of having that power is exciting. Plus, power also associates itself closely with money. And who doesn't like money? That's why I hear people study management, because management pays well. However, maybe that's not the case when we think about leadership and the power that we bestow upon those we consider leaders.

Maybe the search for power and the way that we use the word *leadership* has skewed the way we view leadership and what it indeed is. Moreover, this is where the lines between management and leadership got crossed. Our desire to lead could stem from feeling the need to help those around us and those whom we work with. Whatever the reason, or reasons, may be, the most important is the one to you.

Think to yourself and add on to your definition:

▸ How do you define leadership?

▸ What attributes, skills, and behaviors make a leader, a leader?

▸ Why did you buy this book? What are you looking to change in your life with your leadership and why?

▸ Why do you want to be a leader? Are you a leader now regardless of where you are in your career?

▸ Why is being a leader or working on your leadership ability vital to you now?

No one can tell you how to define leadership. No one can tell you what leadership is and what it isn't. No one can answer these questions—the only person who can is you. That's the beauty of leadership. It's fluid. It's what we make it and why. Defining it depends on what we want to achieve as leaders and how we assign a value to others who lead.

There is no perfect definition. In creating our own definition and gaining clarity on what leadership is to us, it gives us perspective. Knowing this, we can then define how we will move forward with our decisions and if being a leader is the best decision for us. Answering these questions builds our foundation in moving forward and how we assess the value of others in what we want and need.

When I began to define leadership for myself and in considering its value in people who lead, I realized that one word kept coming to mind: *initiative*. Leaders don't wait to be told. They act. They decide to lead. Initiative, to me, is what defines leadership. Here is a more formal definition in how I define leadership:

> A leader is a person with drive and purpose who takes the initiative to act while inspiring, engaging, and motivating others in achieving goals toward a shared vision.

This is my definition, though. Use it to help guide you, but consider what leadership means to you and why. That will be your foundation in how you make your leadership decisions in moving forward and applying concepts from this book to your life.

Redefining Leadership

Before evaluating the value in leadership, let's dig deeper into our definitions and understanding. No one's definition is wrong and there is no right answer, but maybe we have some underlying bias and misconceptions in whom we define as leaders that are worth addressing.

A specific story comes to mind. One day at work, while I was walking down the hall, I noticed the company's CEO running toward the men's room. I thought to myself: he must have diarrhea.

Now, that may sound utterly ridiculous, as it should, but it struck me as incredibly human to see him in that situation. Why? It made him seem human and not some sort of CEO pillar that made him unapproachable. We do this with our leaders. We put them on pedestals and make them seem unattainable with the lists of skills, the traits, the behaviors, and the comparisons to others. We take away much of their humanness.

How? We can't say certain things for fear of angering them. We can't act a certain way for fear of changing their perceptions of us (hey, we want to look perfect to the CEO). We can't treat them the way that we would treat our peers or colleagues. They are far too mighty and superior. We can't be honest. We can't be ourselves. We can't trust.

CEOs are humans. VPs are humans. People managers are humans. For some reason, we forget that and idolize them. Organizations forget that and encourage that forgetfulness. We all need to be perfect and professional each day, all day. However, even CEOs get diarrhea.

I was perusing LinkedIn after writing this section. Feeling somewhat ridiculous about talking about the link from diarrhea to vulnerability to the importance of vulnerability to leadership, I was struck by a "liked" post that happened upon my feed.

This person wrote: "I can't stop thinking about our company meeting yesterday. In my experience, it's rare to see an exec (much less a cofounder) be open, vulnerable, and honest about difficult topics. We are lucky to have a leadership team that leans in when it gets hard, not shy away from what's difficult, and be transparent with the team."

We don't teach vulnerability when we teach management. We teach strength. We teach theory. We teach managing numbers. This is what wraps management in a different box and bow. Leadership is about being human and, at times, means showing our vulnerability to others as a way to connect. When we connect, we lead.

We have titles. We have titles at jobs. We can have that title and job today, but it doesn't mean we will have it tomorrow. Whether it be school, work, life—whatever. It's a title. A title doesn't define who we are as people and as leaders. We do that through our actions and behaviors, which are based on our decisions of what we decide to do, or not.

It also means that we can't fear people in titles. And if we do have a title, it doesn't rip the humanness and vulnerability out of us when working with other people Keep that in mind as we move through the rest of the text. CEOs are people. Leaders are people. And people get diarrhea. People can be vulnerable. People make decisions.

Now, knowing that vulnerability is a part of leadership, let's debunk more stereotypes in our definitions to challenge our biases and misperceptions about leadership so we can better frame our decisions through enhancing our awareness. This will help to free our inhibitions that may be holding us back from deciding to lead.

The Forty-Something, White, Male VP

One day, I took a drive to Cape Cod and thought about every piece of my career from my commute to my struggles to my coworkers to my once failed promotion to my future and to my successes. I thought about where I was and where I wanted to go. I thought about the people I worked with and the things that I did. In some ways, I felt proud. I don't know why on that one afternoon I decided to reassess, but I did.

In those thoughts, I realized that I had devoted myself and my career to making forty-something, White men who were in corporate leadership roles happy. I let these CEOs dictate how I found value both in myself and my work because of their title as leader. I gave up my personal life, worked hard, cried, and based my happiness on whether or not these men were happy with my work performance and in my defining my value as a leader and as a person. I don't think that I'm alone in that. But then I was struck with this thought: How did this happen?

Once having this realization, I read a lot of career statistics and headlines about the workplace and about gender. These show, as we may already presume, that—

▶ The average CEO age is fifty-six, and the average chief financial officer and chief operating officer is fifty-two.

▶ Only 19 percent of US congressional members, less than 5 percent of Fortune 500 CEOs, and only 2 out of the then-current crop of US presidential candidates are women.

▶ By race, Whites made up the majority of the labor force (79 percent). Blacks and Asians made up an additional 12 percent and 6 percent, respectively.

In looking at those data, it made sense that I had fallen victim to the attack of this ever-prominent species lurking in the halls and coffee areas of corporate office buildings waiting to unleash their unwelcome feedback about *my* job performance and life. This also taught me something fundamental about leadership that we fail to address:

▶ Leadership is not an age.

▶ Leadership is not a gender.

▶ Leadership is not an ethnicity.

Leadership is about people and what they can do. Yet, we follow and judge leaders on age, gender, and ethnicity. Regardless of the other leadership books, articles, courses, and the like on the topic, we need to have a reality check. Men hire other men who are like them and grant them smart-sounding titles such as Senior Director of Financial

Success or Vice President of Emerging Markets. These types see another man, also forty-something, and also White, and think, "Yes, this is someone I can trust. They look like me. They act like me. They are me."

This situation is changing, but not fast enough. We still define and discriminate and make decisions when defining and finding value in leaders and in making our own decisions about our leadership ability. We all have a bias. Moreover, we have a bias about leaders. We need to admit that if we are ever going to change our minds and the minds of those around us.

We need to think about this and how it impacts our decisions especially when it comes to bias about those in leadership, whom we place in leadership roles, and whom we deem worthy to lead. What can we do with this awareness to combat bias to enable us as leaders? Consider that first step: awareness. Once becoming aware that we all have bias, we can make better decisions about ourselves and others as it relates to our leadership and practice. Let's dissect further why we need more diversity in leadership.

Leadership Is Not an Age

Jacob, at sixteen, needed to get a job. However, Jacob was a special guy. No regular teenage job of flipping burgers, scooping ice cream, or taking tickets at the amusement park would do. Jacob met a buddy when he was ten, Nathan, through the Big Brothers and Big Sisters program. The two were inseparable. Nathan participated in a lengthy bike ride in Massachusetts once a year called the Pan-Mass Challenge to raise money for cancer research. In knowing that Jacob needed a job and that Nathan needed to raise several thousands of dollars to participate in this annual bike ride, the duo came up with a brilliant idea.

That idea was to open a pedicab business for Jacob to manage over the summer months, which in turn would help Nathan raise the funds he needed to participate in the bike ride. Talking to the government officials of the small city that they planned to launch their idea in was the first step. Then, through working with local businesses, they ensured sponsorship and support. From that support, they were able to purchase the pedicabs. The two were busy creating and leading a company that wowed tourists and brought locals home safely.

As things started to move forward, the local media outlets began to feature stories about Nathan and Jacob both sharing the friendship between the two while promoting their upcoming business partnership and encouraging locals to keep an eye out for the cabs in the summer months. Then came the next challenge. Who would drive the pedicabs that now had sponsorship, approval to hit the streets, and a well-written mission statement?

The two business partners began advertising for help and assumed that young, well-built, college-aged men would apply to maintain their ripped physiques from riding a bike with a sustainable amount of weight on the back while allowing them to make some money and to meet some ladies during summer break. However, these young academics failed to apply in droves as assumed. Who applied instead? Men in their forties and fifties as a way to get out of the house. A few young people applied. They came and went. However, a solid group of the middle-agers stayed on throughout the six-year duration of the business.

What's the point of this example? When people think about leadership, they tend to think about the experience. Let's face it: when we think of experience, we think age. How many years have they been doing a job, which translates to how old are they? If someone at twenty-eight years of age who had begun working in marketing at eighteen applied for a director-level job at an organization that required ten years of experience, would they get it? Maybe they would. Perhaps they wouldn't.

Ageism is alive and well within today's workplace and applies to the way we look at and define leadership. Older people don't want to be led by younger people, and younger people think that older people are out of the loop. The workplace today is a mishmash of generations and with that comes a vast melting pot of values and wants from work and from leadership from the boomers to the millennials.

In the pedicab situation, Jacob began his leadership path at around sixteen with the start of the business. Jacob and

Nathan could have easily laughed off the idea of starting a pedicab business in the local community. In reality, that's a lot of work for a teenager even with a friend.

But they worked through it. Day after day, decision after decision, the two worked to create and mold this idea into reality, and from that Jacob began to demonstrate his raw abilities to be a leader. Nathan could have easily pushed Jacob aside and taken the reins of the business while only giving Jacob the roles and responsibilities of scheduling, washing the cabs, and refilling soft bike tires. As a leader of this business, Jacob was quiet, yet determined.

He motivated his staff about the mission of the company and checked on them throughout their shifts to ensure they had water, food, or a break in the warm summer New England temperatures. The staff were treated fairly concerning scheduling and the work was spread out to ensure that one person didn't get every weekend night shift.

Even though Jacob was deemed leader by Nathan, people respected him as one regardless of that official title concerning the business. He was, after all, young when working as a manager of the pedicab service. The staff could have easily contacted and worked with Nathan instead of Jacob if they saw age and level of experience as a problem or barrier to the company's success. But they didn't. They saw Jacob as a leader. They didn't see him as a sixteen-year-old when it came to the business. Was he a perfect leader? No. Is anyone?

Jacob acted as a leader who helped his staff do well, and the business grew in popularity, expanded to new locations, and gained revenue, thus helping Nathan achieve his goal of riding the cancer fundraising bike ride. Leadership isn't an age. This example shows us that.

Leadership is having an opportunity and the ability to prove yourself, as Jacob did, through your decisions, initiative, and behaviors. Real leadership shines through outside of a corporate title or years of experience. It's about who we are as people and what we can accomplish while working and collaborating with others.

Leadership Is Not a Gender

In being a woman and one who has hosted women's leadership groups, conferences, and networking sessions, I would fail myself and those I've helped if I didn't include discussion around gender, regardless of how you self-identify, and leadership, especially in thinking about the forty-something, White male VP.

Have you ever noticed that leadership books are geared to the masses or geared to women specifically? We don't see *Leadership for Men* gracing the shelves. We do see book after book about ways that women can enhance their financial status, assertiveness, and leadership ability all while looking and dressing the part.

Leadership is not a gender. Leadership is leadership. It doesn't, and shouldn't, matter if you are a man or a woman in a leadership role. People are leaders. People are leaders regardless of what gender they are. In understanding our bias, further understanding diversity and inclusion is essential in today's workplace and to leadership, as we see often in the news, on social media, and in our workplaces. It's something we can make decisions about in trying to challenge ourselves and our bias.

Regardless of the statistics, the comments that men make about women still amaze me—about women's age, dress, looks, intelligence, marital status, and children status—even today when it comes to judging their ability to lead. I once heard a story about a woman in a leadership role within a sales organization. And, at one point, her husband and her boss met. In front of her, the two began to talk about her work performance and ability to lead.

Think about that: her husband and her boss talked about her leadership ability and work performance right in front of her as if she wasn't even there and like that was okay. Think about the decisions that each person made in this scenario whether conscious or not in considering bias. If you don't see something wrong, or at least questionable, with this and how we define leadership and those who lead, consider taking the Implicit Association Test (IAT) on Gender-Career (https://implicit.harvard.edu/implicit/).

This tool is helpful in measuring and then understanding how you may not be aware of your bias with gender (or with other types of bias toward people). The tool can be a simple step in navigating if bias is impacting you as a leader and how you define leadership in others. Let's bring this back to gender, however. Women have different decisions to make about their leadership than men. Men also can make decisions about how they work with and understand the issues that are important to women within the workplace and in life.

Who knows if women and men will ever be truly equal when we define each as leaders and within the workplace. This discussion has been happening now for hundreds of years. It will continue for hundreds more if we don't start acting now to change that conversation and change the landscape through our decisions, by understanding our bias, and examining how we define and find value in those who lead.

We can't wake up and make the same decisions about ourselves as leaders and for the development of others when it comes to leadership and gender. We can decide to gain insight into ourselves on our bias (awareness), practice better and more inclusive Leadership Lifestyle (practice, as explained later in this book), and obtain feedback on this from those around us (evaluation). Sometimes these biases are deeply rooted. We can make these decisions to change for ourselves, exemplify those decisions to those we lead, and teach our children to move beyond these for the sake of a better future for all.

Leadership Is Not an Ethnicity

I career coached a Japanese-American woman who was in her midthirties and a mother who was driven and smart. Let's call her Sigu. When I first met and started working with her, she reported to an Indian-American male, Jai, in his forties and was getting promoted and acknowledged often and had recently been granted a formal people manager role. Jai also gave her flexibility to balance long working hours with motherhood. She loved her job and enjoyed her life.

Jai was a great leader and manager from what Sigu said. She admired how he talked about his vision and drive and how he built a strong team that collaborated well among each other and with other teams across the company. She also appreciated that he was like her and nonwhite. All was right with the world.

A few months into our time together, the organizational structure changed, and she went from reporting to Jai to reporting to a forty-something, White male, Harry. Once making that change, her world changed dramatically. She and Harry didn't get along. He claimed she wasn't a hard worker. Harry demoted her from a people manager role and took projects away from her. He even got to the point of accusing her of not being passionate enough and attributed that to her being a mother due to not being fully focused on the job. The other people on the team were two White women and two men: one who was White and one who was Afghan.

These four were younger, unmarried, and had no children. Harry raved about them and made sure each had what he or she needed to do well in his or her roles, but not Sigu. Sigu didn't change in those few short months. What changed was whom she reported to. She went from loving her job to having panic attacks and seeking medical attention to deal with the stress and anxiety that she now faced with a new manager.

As Sigu began to sunset out of the company, Harry focused his attentions on the Afghan man whom he started to say things about: doesn't work hard enough, can't do the job, for example. Now, each person will read this story in different ways. You may see a level of bias toward both gender and ethnicity. You may not. You may think that you have no prejudice against anyone.

Moreover, if you are in a position where you do promote and make hiring decisions, it's important to give this much thought. People may think they are open-minded and unbiased, but are you? Sigu reported to a minority manager at first and had all the opportunity she wanted. She was even being granted a formal leadership role within the organization. All of that changed when she began reporting to someone else. Now, this new manager may not have had any bias against her ethnicity, and all of this grief might have been coincidental. Alternatively, maybe he did, and this was a way to push her out and then try to oust the Afghan man. With this change, she suffered. Her career suffered. Her life suffered.

Bias may be clouding our decisions whether we realize it or not. But in knowing this, we can begin to become more aware and then empowered in how we make decisions about working and hiring others. It helps us to destroy further the barriers that still impede the working world today. An article in the *New York Times* in 2017 illustrates this point:

> Christopher Cabrera, the chief executive of Xactly, understands the challenge of inherent bias. Earlier in his career, he had to hire eight team members.
>
> When he was halfway through the process, his boss, who was African-American, pointed out that the first four hires were all White, 23-year-old men.
>
> "I was so embarrassed because I certainly hadn't done that on purpose," Mr. Cabrera said. The lesson he learned was that we often do what makes us comfortable.
>
> "I distinctly remember [my boss] saying to me: 'How interesting do you think your team meetings will be when you have 12 guys that are 23 years old, White, with the same background? Do you think that that's going to be a challenging and rich environment where you're learning?' So I remember thinking: 'Yeah, that's crazy. Why would I want that?' It stuck with me."

What does this story tell us? It tells us that bias happens whether we realize it or not. This is why I call this out in thinking about this section. Leadership is not skin color. Leadership is about people. Leaders and organizations hurt themselves and their people when they don't include people with diverse backgrounds and cultures. New perspective brings better business decisions. Working with people who can challenge us and our own leadership decisions helps us to become better leaders.

Richness in diversity brings a new perspective. Countless studies show this. Here's another story. I heard this in graduate school from one of my peers, and it has stuck with me throughout the years. There was a gentleman in the class from Ethiopia named Bruk. He was brilliant and very driven. Bruk first came to the United States as a young adult and began interviewing for pharmaceutical leadership positions.

During one interview that was with a woman (the rest were with men), he avoided making eye contact as it was a sign of respect based on his cultural background. When sharing the story, he mentioned that during the interview he didn't give this much thought. After getting the job, he somehow got the interview notes from those who interviewed him. In reading through, he came across the notation from the woman.

In her notes, she wrote that she didn't think he could be trusted as he couldn't make eye contact, and she didn't recommend him for the job. He almost missed this opportunity because of a cultural misunderstanding. Was this a mix of her misreading his actions or was this an ethnicity issue? Alternatively, a combination of both? He went on to move up in the organization and held various leadership roles and did well for himself.

This story does show how we judge. We judge on ethnicity. We judge cultural norms. We need to be aware of these nuances when we define leadership and whom we value as a leader. It is not about the skin color or what country we come from. It's how we decide to lead and behave that enables us to lead. Once understanding and internalizing that, we may be surprised to see leaders where we didn't see leaders before.

I've Picked on the Forty-Something, White Male VP Enough

There's nothing truly wrong with forty-something, White male VPs. Do not run in fear when encountering this person in the hallway. We all have the power to lead regardless of who we are or where we are in our life: twenties, thirties, female, male, trans, White, Black, Asian. Whatever. We can all be leaders.

This perception is changing in business and in the world, bit by bit, day by day. However, it needs to improve more. We have the power to make that decision by deciding now about our leadership ability regardless of who we are. We can also use this increased awareness to face our own bias in our decisions of how we define and categorize leaders. In one study, researchers found that people used factors in photos like gender and face length to make guesses about people's height and then used these same factors when they judged their leadership qualities.

I think about this and how much easier life would be if we all walked outside of our homes in hazmat suits when dealing with other people whether it be at work, volunteering, or heading a community project. Imagine if we couldn't decipher gender. We couldn't decipher age. We couldn't decipher ethnicity. We would follow and lead not giving these factors any thought—not defined by any of these barriers that we put around leaders and ourselves. Give this idea some consideration as you examine your definition, both written and unwritten.

What's Right with How We Define Leadership

Now that we've talked about how we define leadership, how we have overglorified leaders, and ways we should reconsider the way we think about who can lead, let's take a moment to address the positives in the way we define leadership before looking at how we derive value.

Corporations are creating leadership development programs to aid those in people manager roles learn how to be more effective and how to lead. We see academia changing the focus from that of management programs to leadership in recognizing and appreciating this shift and ever-growing need. We see schools including leadership early on in the curriculum to teach all students about the importance of leadership. We read books and articles and listen to webinars and podcasts and radio shows and watch TV where people are talking more about leadership as a whole. We are talking about it. We are finding ourselves trying to learn more from corporations, consultants, academia, and one another.

We are defining leadership and not leaving it up to someone else to do so. We see the value that this study can have for corporations, communities, and, most importantly, our self-study to enhance our development and grow. The last part is the crucial piece for both you and me: What can we do as individuals to improve our leadership ability? How do we use our decisions to do this?

Only we know our history, our situations, our feelings and thoughts, our goals and our lives. This is where we have power. We can think about what we want and make decisions on how to achieve. We can become aware through any of the noted channels (again, media, academia, books, and the like), and we can use those around us to learn more about how these people perceive and experience us and, in knowing that, figure out through our brand exercises how we can define whom we want to be as leaders.

In having this level of awareness, we can then decide to practice. We can practice being good leaders at home. We can practice leadership at work. We can find other ways to lead in our lives from working in the community to starting a side hustle to help us to develop and grow. This is what's right. We can practice and begin to live life as a leader. In doing that, we can start to evaluate in both our self-study and internal reflection through that of meditation or yoga or journaling or seeing changes in the way that people work and interact with us. Evaluation can help our practice and success by gaining feedback outside of ourselves through the insight of people that we trust and value.

In working and talking to people who interact with us, we can use the A/P/E Model cycle again with learning and gaining that awareness on how to keep going or what else to improve. I will talk about this more later on. Learning as a leader never ends. This is not a onetime management class that you can check the box and, boom, you are a management expert. It does not work like that. Not at all.

This is why we need to realize and understand what to think about and where we can go next with our leadership practice and our lifestyle. That's what makes leadership and talking about it fun. Inspiring. Utterly frustrating at times. However, influential, all at the same time. This is your decision. This is your practice. Decide to be aware. Decide to practice. Decide to evaluate.

Decide for yourself to become a leader and take the initiative to act. Know that realizing this and changing the way we lead and define others who do is what's right. This is what's right.

The Leadership Value

Once defining and then redefining, we can begin to see what we value when it comes to leaders and leadership both for our development and in how we interpret the value of others. Let's examine values in the broader sense before narrowing down to why this matters to our leadership decisions. Most people find value in something. We all have our definition of what value means to us and why we value what we do.

Often, when we hear the word *value*, associations with that of religion come to mind. That can be one stream of value in how we define its paths. Also, it's not to say that religious values aren't necessary and relevant. They are. However, there are more to values than religion. We are busy with our own respective lives and allot time to what we value. Life and what we make of it is about prioritization. We prioritize based on our values. Let's look at a few examples.

Maybe we value family or friends or freedom. We could value health or money or career. We can even consider values outside of these buckets and into combinations that help us define our lives, our wants, our paths along with who we are and whom we want to be. We may not always associate values in thinking about how we make decisions and especially how we make decisions about our leadership. But we should.

Leadership values and finding value in leadership is essential. It sets a baseline for how we lead. It also defines what we value in leaders. We do this whether we realize it or not. Think about politicians you follow and admire. Well-suited, smiling, talking heads trying to broadly address how they are similar to us with the same values in blanketed ways to appeal to the masses. We are drawn to some and define them as leaders, while others repulse us and we belittle their ability without having ever experienced them directly.

At work, we talk about values too—leadership, organizational, and cultural. The values we have at work and in the cultures that we work within impact how we make decisions in those settings, or why we work where we do. Think about what you value in your life. Think about what you value at work. Think about what you value about leadership. Now think of three leaders whom you interact with on a regular basis. Do the values you have about your life and work align with those whom you see value in when leading? Let's say we value excellent communication skills in our work leaders.

▶ Do we appreciate great communication outside of our work lives? Do you care if your aunt or cousin writes a robust, well-written email to you on a Saturday?

▸ Do you judge your child's potential leadership ability based on how they give visionary speeches at the dinner table if you are home for dinner?

▸ Do you reprimand your friends if they are late to a lunch gathering and note their failure in providing a well-thought-out agenda? Or do you appreciate them for their honesty, empathy, and vulnerability?

Probably no. If you do, you likely drive them crazy. But this is how we define value within leaders in the modern day. Why? Why aren't we in a place where we define and value leaders inside the workplace the same way that we identify and value leaders outside of the workplace? Classes, articles, and tools focus on value both in finding and defining from an organizational or corporate world standpoint. Even leadership consultants and trainers who ask people to perform exercise after exercise ask those eager to lead to think about what they value and why.

They pose questions like these:

▸ What life events or happenings have helped to shape you?

▸ What were you taught as a child when it came to values and how did that form you as an adult?

▸ What do you value and why? In your life? In your work? In your heart?

Some of us can give this type of exercise serious thought in defining life happenings and how said incidents helped to shape who we are. Same with defining family and our upbringing in the way we were raised and how this relates to our values as people and as leaders. Others may have more of a difficult time giving thought to their upbringing, life events, and values and how that has impacted who they are at this very moment. I've heard that some think this is too "mushy" or "touchy-feely" for the workplace or when thinking about leadership or management.

We'll discuss this more in thinking about our Leadership Lifestyle as it's important to see where alignment is in what we value, what we appreciate in leadership, and whom we value as leaders to unite the concepts to help us with our own leadership decisions. Once in a course, I had a student, Mike, ask me about this in great detail with a touch of anger and frustration in his voice. He was confused about why we were talking about values when talking about leadership and career. I knew him within a marketing and product management role at a software organization.

Mike was in his sixties and had worked at this organization for more than thirty years. From the mix of tenure and age, he would spend his sun-setting career years at the same organization and in the same role. He was happy with that. When answering my question about values, he explained that he didn't know how to define his values and what that would even mean to the workplace and why that matters to how we interpret the significance of leaders both for ourselves and for those in "formal" leadership roles.

I asked him to name one value. Just one simple value. Mike took a few moments to think and then replied, "Hard work."

Fair enough. I pressed on. "Why did you think of hard work?" I asked, trying to dig deeper into his mind.

Mike thought again for a few moments and then looked up at me and said, "My father was a hard worker, and when I was a child, he always told me that hard work was important in life. I always worked hard throughout my life and then started working here. I never decided to leave after the decades that I've been here and will continue to work hard."

A valid value. I explained to him that if hard work were a value even outside of the walls of this office, — if he gets a new job post-retirement, let's say working at a golf course, — he'd still value hard work and he'd probably still be a hard worker within that role. He nodded and agreed. The look on his face showed that he began to internalize this lesson once he was able to frame it based on the lesson he learned from his father.

The next step for Mike would be to further define these values in how he defines value about his own leadership ability and that of others. In thinking about this, both overall and with this example, we can see how what we value shapes who we are and how we go about our lives day to day. We make decisions about our lives and our leadership based on our values.

If we value hard work and leaders who are hard workers, that's a value in how we can further define leadership for both ourselves and how we evaluate others. I challenge you to think about your values and how they relate to your definition. Religious, personal, work, whatever you think of value, think of that value and how you came to that conclusion. Your values will determine your decisions about the way you lead. Your values define how you define leaders and leadership. Your values define your life and what you want out of it.

Once defining leadership and further dissecting it to find value within that definition, we can use this as the foundation of our leadership practice and development decisions. When thinking about your values and what they mean to you and how they were developed within you through life happenings, childhood, and other moments, you can further build your mindset and decision-making about your leadership through this self-awareness. This is one step in gaining awareness as part of the A/P/E Model that we can then use to make decisions about our leadership.

2

The Leadership Brand

The Massachusetts Institute of Technology (MIT) is a popular place. It has been the stage for many movies, such as *Good Will Hunting* and *A Beautiful Mind*. Oh yeah, it's a pretty terrific school for the world's brightest minds too. Not only is MIT a popular spot for the world's, academics first-time in undergraduate school, but its graduate program is also special.

A lot of great ventures and partnerships that have changed the world have come out of MIT. But what does MIT have to do with leadership, let alone creating a Leadership Brand? Well, a lot. As we start thinking about our Leadership Brand, let's first look at another popular and useful marketing term: *personas*.

Personas

In thinking about partnerships turned into successful ventures coming out of MIT, the story was told at an annual marketing conference that Brian Halligan and Dharmesh Shah met at MIT's Sloan School of Management during their graduate study. "Who are they?" you're probably asking. They are the founders of HubSpot. HubSpot is a marketing platform that's gained much popularity over the years due to its functionality in both the platform itself and through customer training.

One word that comes up in the marketing world is *personas*. Building on the teachings of the HubSpotology, personas are fictional, generalized characters that encompass the various needs, goals, and observed behavior patterns among a company's real and potential customers.

Creating personas is a valuable practice in marketing as doing so ensures that marketing tactics are in line with those people that marketing leaders are trying to target with their efforts to take some action—like buying a product or service. When I worked in marketing, I spent much time thinking and developing these fictional personas and how each aided in the effectiveness of my marketing campaigns. In other words, who would be most impacted by which content and campaigns, and why?

I began thinking like these people. I started making decisions like these people. I felt like I had become these people. When I changed careers from marketing to leadership development, I kept thinking about personas; however, I transitioned from thinking about personas concerning marketing to that of leadership. I also began to think about myself in relation to personas. I wasn't the same person, or the same persona that I had been in marketing.

Catherine as the marketing manager persona needed to be focused on data and trends, bringing in revenue and motivating those in sales to push products. The marketing Catherine persona wasn't one that I loved being. I didn't find value in it. I didn't feel like a leader. I hated the work. I even hated myself sometimes. Catherine in the leadership development persona needed to be warm and approachable, able to connect with people and flexible to employee needs. The leadership development Catherine persona felt more like me and who I was as a person. It fit my values, and I felt like a leader. Plus, I liked who I was.

Both of these career personas required that I be hard-working, driven, and dedicated. Regardless of industry, these were still core to who I was as a person and as a professional. The Catherine outside of work persona was a good friend, a bit lazy at housecleaning and texting back plus a bit too sarcastic for some. However, still hard-working, driven, and dedicated, although sometimes the dishes do stay in the sink a day or two longer than they should.

In knowing myself and trying to define my own overarching Leadership Brand, I had to give thought to my various personas and what each told me about myself. Who were my personas that created me as a leader? What did that mean to the way that I lead and to whom I was in relation to my own decisions? I gave much thought to how people know professional Catherine vs. personal Catherine.

Was there a difference, or not? How could I unite my various personas to think about both and why does this matter to my Leadership Brand overall? Before looking into this more and why you should start thinking about and defining your leadership personas and in keeping with the thread of marketing, let's talk brands and how we represent ourselves in the way that we lead.

The Brand

Brands in the marketing and communication sense can be fun to talk about. Thinking about questions like, "Why do we buy what we buy?" or "Why do we eat where we eat?" and "Why do we trust the companies we do?" can be an interesting debate and exercise in self-awareness. Why do we buy paper towel A over paper towel B? Maybe we think A works better than B.

Alternatively, maybe we were also sucked into buying due to the brand name of paper towel A promising better absorbing ability than B, so that's what we buy. We may not realize that brands and what they promise, like great leaders, can suck us in with their stories, their visions, and their aspirations for better things and better lives.

In creating a new brand for a marketing client, the company I was working for was seeking the services of a branding company in Cambridge, Massachusetts. See? A popular place. Some of the questions that these brand experts asked were about what our client's brand story was, what we were trying to accomplish with a new brand, and, my favorite, if our brand was a celebrity, who would it be and why?

Branding and personas—oh my! So what does this have to do with leadership? When we think about ourselves as leaders and how we want to live and lead, we should complete a similar practice and exercise. We need to define our personas in thinking about who we are at work, who we are at home, and who we are as a person, overall. In answering, we can begin to create our Leadership Brand. With that brand, we can further define our mission and our story. This aligns back with where we started: How do we define leadership and, from that definition, find value when it comes to leadership? Think of the process as similar to how we describe the value of the brands that we buy and trust, how we want people to explain us and our value as leaders.

We see corporations and organizations completing this exercise to help market and to position their status. We can, and should, do the same. Creating this profile for ourselves can help us clarify what we want and how we want to lead. This is our foundation for our decisions and a compass in how we determine when we act and take initiative as leaders.

This is the basis we need to first create for ourselves in moving forward with the concept of making decisions about being a leader, integrating the A/P/E Model and living a Leadership Lifestyle, which I discuss in further detail in coming chapters. This also helps us to market ourselves and our leadership, so others perceive our value as leaders. A Leadership Brand conveys your identity and distinctiveness as a leader. It communicates your value. It tells your story. It showcases your decisions.

Your Leadership Story

Now that you are thinking about your personas and your brand, let's talk about stories. When was the last time you read or heard a story? When was the last time you read an organization's "About Us" or "Our Story"?

For stories, maybe you recently heard one on NPR. Or perhaps you watched a TED Talk or had lunch with a coworker or friend. Maybe you were interviewing with a new company and wanted to understand the organization in better detail. Or perhaps you read for a school project for research or to understand the importance of these statements. Two stories came to mind for me.

The first. I once worked with a woman who had the mission statement of the company that we worked for printed out and taped right below her computer monitor. When I asked her why, she noted that every time she turned her computer on, picked up the phone, or answered an email, the note would remind her of the bigger picture of why she was doing what she was doing and why it mattered to the organization's brand and mission.

I was impressed. I had never thought about doing that before. Another place that I worked had a concise mission statement. In staff meetings, the CEO would ask people to recite it on call during the staff meetings. Everyone had to know it, and everyone had to know it by heart. When we first began looking at personas and brands, I talked about how Brian Halligan and Dharmesh Shah founded HubSpot after meeting at MIT. I also talked about how this story is shared at a marketing conference.

HubSpot organizes that conference annually, and at each event, the two leaders share some story about the company to create a sense of community, to provide updates to their customers as needed about new value adds to the product, and to humanize both themselves and the organization as a whole. Now, on HubSpot's website, the organization further supports the need and value of stories by having a section on their About Us page called "The Story Behind Our Story."

People love stories. I love stories. I'm sure that you probably like stories too. This is not new. Storytelling is not only essential to uniting people in business, manipulating us into trusting certain brands, and helping us to connect with others, but also to join us under the leadership of those people who have mastered the art. Our personas tell us stories about ourselves—who we are at work, who we are at home, and who we are overall.

That overall part tells us about our brand. Understanding that brand and our personas also helps us to figure out who we are as people and as leaders. Having that understanding helps us see our lives in a new light. In that glow, we can write our own leadership story, or mission, to then use when communicating our value to others so then they also perceive us as leaders based on our decisions. These three elements further strengthen the foundation on which you will make your leadership decisions using the A/P/E Model.

Ask yourself:

▸ Who are my personas? At work? At home? Where else?

▸ What characteristics and attributes unite all of my personas?

▸ In knowing characteristics and attributes, how would I use these to create and define the value of my Leadership Brand?

▸ In thinking about how I defined, understood, and analyzed my personas to create my brand, how would I explain my leadership value through story to others?

You are the only one who can answer these questions in thinking about your leadership and your lifestyle. This creates your foundation on which you can make your leadership decisions.

Answering will enable you to look historically at your path while also looking ahead to your goals and aspirations and how you want to be perceived. Later, we'll examine the idea that "perception is reality" and how to tie these concepts together so you can make better leadership decisions.

I have my MBA students attempt something similar as their first self-analysis on leadership. They need to define what a Leadership Brand is, talk about their Leadership Brand, and share a leadership story that exemplifies how they live their brand. When they first learn about the assignment, they say, "This sounds so easy! Why would you assign this to us?" But then they start it and they struggle. It's hard to do. It challenges them to think about their own behaviors and decisions as leaders. But the feedback, once completed, is often positive.

Troy is a former student of mine who explained to me how beneficial he found this assignment. Troy never felt like a leader, but once he was able to define his Leadership Brand and think about times he led with his leadership story, it clicked for him. He was leading whether he realized it or not. Try this exercise for yourself in summarizing:

1. Define what Leadership Brand means to you in a few words.

2. Outline your personas—think work, home, school, community—and the values and goals of each.

3. Write a summary of two to three paragraphs on what your Leadership Brand is, including how your personas support your brand.

4. Draft a story of a time that you led and exemplified the attributes of your Leadership Brand to clarify your leadership story.

As a word of caution, don't rush through this exercise. I've sat through plenty of courses where people were asked to complete similar exercises, and they rushed through them for the sake of completing a class and then were encouraged to complete them on their own at a later time and never do so. That's your own decision in finding value, or not, in this type of practice. Some see this type of thing as too fluffy. Maybe you do, but perhaps you don't. Books and exercises and courses and practices and assessments like this are tools. Let's say someone gave you a hammer, some nails, and some wood and instructed you to make a box. You could sit there and make the box or not. It's up to you if you use the tools and items given to you to make something with them or not. Not anyone else. It's your decision.

Share what you wrote with those around you. That can be intimidating as you may feel concern for what those whom you share this with may say or think about you. You may have insecurity sneak in and think, "What if this person thinks this is stupid and doesn't see me as a leader?" Stop that type of thinking. I know that may be easier said than done, but there's only so much you can do on your own for your development. Sharing this with people around you can help you to refine what you've written and possibly add some more clarity to what you are already doing and how you can further clarify your goals.

Plus, sharing with those around you at work can open the door for more feedback from them on the progress you are making in thinking about the E in the A/P/E Model for evaluation, which we will further outline later on. We can't assume that just since we attend a leadership program, read a book, or take a class that it makes us a leader. It doesn't. It's our decisions and actions that make us a leader in all aspects of our life. This brings us to our next concept of living a Leadership Lifestyle.

3

The Leadership Lifestyle

In agreeing that leadership isn't a nine-to-five title within the corporate world only due to the nature of managing people based on a title, it's important to know that leadership and being a leader is a lifestyle. Leadership is a way of living that we establish and guide through our decisions and the creation and basis of our Leadership Brand. The Leadership Lifestyle is a phrase that we will now integrate into thinking about our leadership decisions as we prepare to discuss the A/P/E Model.

As leaders, we should lead by example, meaning that we need to understand and internalize how this trickles into all aspects of our lives. Such thinking creates the foundation of how people define us and how we define others as leaders. It's the foundation of our definition and how we derive value. It's what our brand stems from and becomes.

I've witnessed people in leadership roles within organizations who weren't cut out for it. The skills weren't there, the aptitude toward working with other people wasn't there, and I wondered, "Who saw what in this person that enabled them to move up the corporate chain into a leadership role?" That's a scary thought. Some of these people were lackluster in the workplace and would then come in and talk about their personal lives, which reflected poor choices that impacted their lives overall and their ability to lead (such as binge drinking or other high-risk behaviors).

Who wants to follow someone like that? I worked with a VP, Karen, who fell into all these categories: terrible person and a terrible leader. Karen caused issue after issue with clients, turned people against each other, was a poor communicator, and just overall not that intelligent or self-aware. However, the CEO of this organization thought Karen was amazing. Those who reported to her knew she wasn't amazing at all. In coming to work, Karen always told some story about her bad behavior outside of the office. Stories were unrealistic and made many of us question her life decisions and overall ability to lead. We didn't respect her as a leader based on her lifestyle choices that she unfortunately chose to share with us.

That coupled with her being an asshole (which I will address further on) made her unfollowable. As a team, we complained about Karen, the clients complained about Karen, and the CEO finally changed his perceptions about her, and she was out the door soon after. We judge each other on behaviors and stories like this. We judge, and then we question the individual and their decisions whether we realize it or not.

We determine if we are going to follow these people or whether we are going to make jokes about them in hushed corners of the office with our most trusted colleagues. We make our own decisions if we are going to respect these people and their leadership. People who live lives like this are frustrating when it comes to defining leadership as their choices outside the workplace don't align. This is what makes leadership a lifestyle and not merely a title within a job role or function.

We all make mistakes, though. We're all human. We all can be vulnerable and sometimes we're going to make bad decisions. But, as leaders, we need to have more self-awareness about every word, every behavior, every promise, every action, and every step that we take. Why? Because we're leaders. And leadership is hard. We become and stop being leaders with our decisions as simple or as complex or as ethical or not as they may be with how we lead in our lives.

You don't need to be perfect, but you do need to realize that this is a reality in how we judge ourselves and those around us when we define leadership. The challenge is trying to be human and vulnerable while also being a role model and making decisions that are reflective of who we are. I've heard plenty of stories of simple mistakes that people in formal leadership roles made that triggered those they led to think differently about them. Actions that could have been avoided that would have kept their Leadership Brand and mission strong and trustworthy. Give this story consideration.

A coworker of mine, Suzie, was tall and voluptuous. Her outfits, although professional, were on the sexy side. Susie was a hard worker, and she was a great friend too. She had a presence about her, in any case. Men ogled her even when she wore sweatpants and hoodies. Later on, we'll address some of this further when thinking about timing, opportunity, looks, and likes (the concept I call TOLL) concerning awareness and perception around leadership.

The president of the company that Suzie and I worked for appreciated her hard work. At one point, Suzie and the president went on a trip for a board meeting. To reduce your level of suspense, no, as far as I know, they didn't have an affair. However, after the board meeting, Suzie was going to stay another day to enjoy the area. In knowing that, the president bought Suzie a massage package at the hotel and spa where the board meeting was held and where they were staying. He wanted her to relax and enjoy herself and asked her not to tell anyone about this lavish and, somewhat, intimate gift.

Reading this, you may have different reactions. First, how inappropriate this is. Or, second, not a big deal and how sweet for the boss to buy a subordinate a gift like this to thank her for her hard work.

When Suzie told me this story, the first thing that ran through my head is that they were having an affair, hence the prior warning. My second thought was a level of uneasiness about the situation. After hearing that story, I felt angry and uncomfortable. Those feelings made me think differently about that leader who had been a person whom I admired for a long time. That, coupled with other female employees who mentioned that they were keeping records of what this person said to them, was disconcerting. People talk even if the intentions are well meaning.

From that talk, we create our perceptions, assumptions, and ideas about the storyteller and the person being discussed. It all stems from someone deciding to act or behave in a certain way that may be questionable from a leadership perspective. After hearing this, when I was alone with this man, regardless of how much I had initially respected his leadership ability, I felt myself being scared and shy in trying to avoid any possible issue. I lost trust and began to doubt.

Suzie and the president of the company were a bit too close. And due to their relationship, he bought her a somewhat special gift of a massage. She accepted and then relayed to other people even though she was asked to keep it a secret. Those people talk. Secrets sometimes don't stay secrets. Perceptions based on those decisions are changed, and those perceptions may be irreversible. This is an authentic situation. Moreover, it demonstrates a common issue: leadership is not a moral card that abstains people from their human nature and wants and needs.

Leaders are people after all (heck, they are even people who can get diarrhea.). And when being a leader in the formal sense or wanting to improve yourself as a leader, it's important to be aware of actions like this. Decisions are like dominos. Leaders should show thanks to those around them. But there is a line and that line can vary from person to person in considering what's acceptable versus what's not. We value people and leaders who show appreciation. We appreciate people who treat others in a way that is respectable and honest. Sometimes our intent is different than what's interpreted and may impact our brand. This, too, is something we need to be aware of.

When we see people exhibiting questionable behaviors, we develop opinions about them that go beyond their role within an organization. As people, we then develop opinions about those people that, regardless of their role, impede the way that we view them and if we decide to follow them or not. Moreover, in thinking about following them, it impacts our own decisions if we will or not. It hinders how much we are willing to give and to engage working for someone like that.

This is why thinking about leadership in relation to a lifestyle and to our decisions is essential. In the next chapter, we'll examine everyday decisions that each one of us makes and how even the simplest of decisions can impact our ability to lead. Give thought to this as we move forward to your Leadership Lifestyle. Are you making decisions each day that support it? Are there areas for improvement that can make a more significant impact on your life and path overall? Now that we've thought about ways we can further unite our brand to our value and to our decisions, we can talk about how we use our brain to further make decisions about our leadership practice.

4

Perception Is Reality

During cool, fall Wednesday nights in the Berkshires of Massachusetts, I found myself sitting in an undergraduate classroom looking at pictures of warm places: Turks and Caicos, Bermuda, and Costa Rica. Places I had only dreamed of visiting. I was taking a travel marketing class. The premise was to examine how the travel industry markets its "products" with the products being hotels, flights, and vacation packages to specific personas like singles, couples, families, and seniors.

It was taught by a woman named Stephanie Abrams from Albany, New York, who hosted a travel radio broadcast and focused on the beauty of destinations all over the world and how professionals attract people to destinations. It seemed like Stephanie had been everywhere. She knew what made an excellent travel product. During one class, she brought up a phrase that I, in my twenty-one years of life at that point, had never heard before, but it made more sense than anything I learned. It has proven to be more valuable than I ever thought it would be.

That phrase was this: perception is reality. Perception is reality? What on earth does that mean? It means that your reality is based on your perception. Your perception of the world differs from anyone else's due to your experiences, upbringing, mindset, education, gender, ethnicity, and the list goes on and on. I had not heard this phrase before. She was not the creator of it, either, but she was the one who first woke me to its brilliance.

My perception of the world is my reality. No one else's. Just mine. Think about this. You and your friend start talking to a man named Frank at a restaurant. Frank, to you, is funny and knowledgeable. He discusses his travels around the world through his business ventures as an entrepreneur. After wishing Frank a good night, you and your friend exit the restaurant.

You turn to your friend and say, "Wasn't Frank so beautiful and charismatic? What fun to talk to someone so worldly. I really felt an instant connection with him. Wow, I hope we can connect again soon."

Your friend, on the other hand, rolls her eyes, looks at you with disgust, and begins a tirade. "Are you freaking kidding me? What a pompous ass. How self-centered was that guy? He's so obnoxious. He ruined our evening together. What a bummer."

You're taken aback. "What?"

"Yah," your friend says, "how could anyone just sit there and talk on and on about themselves without coming up for air or ask about the people that they were taking with?"

You are stunned. Speechless.

Now, in this situation, both you and your friend had very different perceptions about Frank based on his attributes. That is your reality, your perception. These perceptions are based on a variety of factors as outlined earlier, but each molded you and your friend's reality about whom Frank was as a person based on how you experienced what he said and how he behaved.

The same applies to leadership. This is what makes defining leaders and leadership insanely tricky as the way we define leadership varies from person to person. It's based on the way that we perceive and experience our world. But we would still experience and make perceptions differently based on who we are. Think back to talking about politicians. One appeals to you, but not to your friend and vice versa.

We all experience leadership differently. I could work for someone and think they are the best leader ever. You could work for that same exact person and think they are the worst leader. It's all about perception. It's about the stories we tell ourselves about leaders and about leadership and the people in these roles and about ourselves as leaders. It's all relative.

But we all can define behaviors and skills that leaders should have to be effective even though we may experience these differently. Some skills can be agreed on. For example, people often note that being skilled at public speaking is an essential trait for leaders. In looking at politicians, who are often considered symbols of leadership, a majority might agree that this politician is a great public speaker—or not.

We can tell an excellent public speaker from a not-so-good public speaker. That's easy and can be agreed upon. Yes, there may be some differences in style and tone that people may have varying opinions on due to their realities about public speaking, but the overall outcome is that people agree this person speaks well in public.

Some people we may perceive as big thinkers and, to us, that translates to leadership. Some may look at those same people and think they are quacks. Whose perception is right? Whose perception is wrong? Organizations look at behaviors and how behaviors roll into competencies and values and what this means to those who can lead from a people management role. In having each defined, this is how organizations and its leaders make decisions on who else can be leaders.

Organizations often frame the development of leadership concerning competencies, or the behavioral skills and areas of knowledge required by the business. However, focusing on competencies alone dismisses the critical role that psychological resources play in leadership—especially in today's fast-paced and uncertain global leadership environment.

Later on, when we look at TOLL, we'll focus on why "likes" matter, to an extent, but it lends itself to this idea of perception and understanding when we think about leadership in both our self and in understanding how we see others. Let's personalize this a bit more. Maybe you've experienced this situation.

Visualize this: You work at an organization where you once flourished, and suddenly a change happens. You start to underperform for whatever reason. Maybe it was a change in you or the way you perceive the role. Remember, perception is reality. You hate the tasks, you hate the people, and you hate the boss. You're failing within the role. You decide to try and ride it out instead of quitting or finding a new job, thinking these feelings will pass.

You start to receive poor feedback and performance reviews and then begin to hate the place even more. You are a rat trapped in a cage clawing desperately to escape, and no matter what you do, or how hard you work, nothing is ever right. As your work suffers, people begin to see you differently. You go from a star employee to the bottom of the barrel.

Your reality is, you hate your job and now your life. People around you begin to perceive you differently. Your reputation begins to suffer. It's a no-win for all. But did the perception change the reality or was the reality truly the reality? Then, one day, you receive a new offer. Finally, you get to move on.

At this new position, they perceive you as a go-getter, a passionate and dedicated employee and someone they want on their team—the exact opposite of what you were before. Your new reality is being that star again. You see it. Your peers see it. Overall, life is good. The best phrase I've heard that relates to this situation is this: happiness in life is goodness of fit.

Were you not an excellent and driven employee before? You could have had it in you. Due to the circumstances you were in, you lost it somehow. Maybe you got bored or didn't connect with the manager. We change. Did that aid in changing your reality? Your perceptions? Yes. Did it change the way that people around you viewed you? Yes.

They didn't know you on a personal level to understand how you honestly felt about the situation, but their entire perception changed based on what they were experiencing when working with you and how they perceived you.

How People Perceive You

In thinking about leadership and being able to make decisions about your leadership and your Leadership Brand, you need to take a moment and step back from your situation, as difficult as that may be, and think about how people perceive you. It can be challenging to do and build this level of self-awareness. This is why gaining awareness through feedback is so important. It challenges you to think about the way you would view you if you were someone else. Think about a situation in your life. Maybe it's work. Maybe it's family. In this situation, you know how you feel, how you act, and what you say.

During a three-day department meeting, I felt myself crashing during the morning of the second day. I hadn't slept the night before and was bogged down from the amount of information that we were being given. I was trying my best to focus, but had moments of slumps.

About a week later, my manager, Hillary, mentioned that one of the top leaders in the room, Mark, noticed my struggle, but perceived it as boredom and not exhaustion. Hillary warned me to be careful and to try to not look so bored next time as to not hurt my career. I was furious at her comment, but the situation illustrated to me why this concept is so important to both career and leadership. Keep this story in mind when we talk about looks later on.

Imagine looking at yourself the way that others do. If you are in a situation where you are unhappy with or are thinking about yourself in this perspective, what's working? What's not? How can you make decisions that would change the situation moving forward that would help to transition to leadership? Stop and think about that. Based on what you know about another person, how would they have interpreted your actions? Your words? In looking at the situation from the point of view of each person involved, how would you view yourself?

Think about that when reflecting on a situation where you did, or did not, lead. Would you be proud? Would you want to follow you? What could you have done differently and how? Moreover, how can you make decisions about that moving forward in understanding perception is the reality?

Assess your reality. Think about the perceptions of how people look at you and how you would look from another person's point of view. How is that impacting how people view you as a leader? How did you see yourself? Use this as a starting point where you may need to gain awareness and then evaluate yourself.

Not only evaluating yourself in your current employment or situation but what can be changed, if anything, to help you further your development and advance your leadership ability. Perception is reality. You can change your reality. You can change perceptions of both your self and those around you. You need to make that decision. You can change people's perceptions of you based on the way you behave and interact with them. And how, in knowing this, we can begin to give more thought to making more precise decisions about our leadership and the way we define and find value in others.

PART II:
The A/P/E Model to Enhance Leadership Decisions

"Watch your thoughts, they become your words.
 Watch your words, they become your actions.
 Watch your actions, they become your habits.
 What your habits, they become your character.
 Watch your character, it becomes your destiny."

Lao Tzu

5

Welcome to the A/P/E Model

I met CJ at a conference. He worked for a telecom giant and was a board member of an association that I was working for. CJ was an influential member of the board. He had the ability to challenge the decisions being made about the association and its strategy. This, matched with his gregarious personality, led to his ability to collaborate and influence people naturally.

One crisp September night in Vancouver during the conference, I joined CJ at a local brewery to talk about what's going on in the industry, what's going on with the conference, and to catch up overall. I liked him as a person and as a leader. Over beers, CJ talked about the conference. His passion for the topic shined through the dim lights of the brewery.

As we talked and savored Canada's most excellent ales, the conversation changed to a side project that CJ had been working on. He was invested in a craft brewery that two of his friends started. I thought his passion showed through before, but now it came to light. As a beer lover, he raved about the quality of the beer and how the brewery would be a gathering place for those in the community.

CJ told me that the cofounders were having disagreements about the business. Due to the conflict and roadblocks with communication and vision for the future between the two, there were only a few months, if that, before the brewery went bankrupt and the significant investment that CJ made would be gone. Needless to say, as an investor and lover of beer, he was angry. And who could blame him? CJ and I talked about him finding new ways to intervene as a friend, an investor, and a leader. He needed to make some very specific decisions quickly if he wanted to protect his friends and his money.

Over the weeks and months following our meeting in Vancouver, CJ began to use his professional expertise and his leadership skills to transform the brewery. To combat issues between the two brewers, he held a moderation session. In that session, he listened to each vent their frustrations. It allowed the brewers to reset the button on their relationship.

Along with working on the relational aspects, CJ then took on the practical task of looking at the current revenue situation as to where they were, where they wanted to go, and how they needed to get there. After his own research to gain more awareness about how the beer industry works, he further defined how they needed to broaden their channels for distribution and increase their production to support those channels.

CJ also learned through his research and networking with other local brewers that money is in the merchandise: think mugs, hoodies, T-shirts, and the like. To drive people buying both the beer and merchandise, he began organizing more events at the brewery. A few months after his dedicated efforts, the brewery began to make a turn for the better. He was evaluating that through sales numbers, the relationship between the two brewers, and feedback they had given him. It wasn't perfect, but the decisions he was making that were also influencing his friends were making a difference to their business and to their relationships.

We can learn several lessons about leadership from this example as we explore the A/P/E Model. First, CJ started by having conversations with those involved to fix the relationships. Those can be the most difficult conversations to have and initiate, but they aid in helping to rebuild trust, discuss points of trouble, and help to make amends. Second, CJ also took the reins by looking at the financials to assess the situation there in line with the relationship issues happening in the background. Third, synching the relationships with the business components enabled him to see the bigger picture and, quickly, rectify the situation.

As a result of his decisions and the initiative he took, things got better. People were drinking the beer, coming to the events, and buying merchandise to wear outside of those walls, generating money and further promoting the brewery through advertising on the clothing. The brewery became successful because someone decided to lead. That's the essence of the A/P/E Model.

We gain **awareness** about ourselves and our situations, we decide to act and **practice** leading and being a leader, and we then **evaluate** our efforts. Leaders don't wait for an invitation. CJ didn't. Entrepreneurs, politicians, business owners, and community leaders who ventured out didn't wait. Leaders are people who decided to act and then followed through with action. This brings us to the second section of the book and an in-depth look into the A/P/E Model and how we can use it to frame our leadership decisions.

Why the A/P/E Model?

After working, teaching, and researching leadership both in the academic and corporate worlds and always asking, What makes a leader, a leader? I had to stop and think about the answer. One day, in preparing for a speech, it hit me. It's a decision, a choice. Someone decides to lead.

Leaders found ways in their life to lead. It doesn't matter how many classes or books or seminars or goals they may have read, attended, or set. If they don't make a decision to lead, they will never be a leader. It's as simple and as hard as that. The A/P/E Model is a cycle that gives us a framework for how we can make decisions and then act on those decisions in changing our behavior to become leaders. It also challenges us to understand and manage the perceptions of those around us and about ourselves.

When talking to executives, managers, and others whom I considered to be leaders from the formal sense in leading people within a company, it became apparent that these people made conscious choices about their careers. They made decisions about how they were going to approach their workday. They made decisions about how they were going to represent themselves. The same applies for those who lead in a nontraditional sense.

They made smart decisions about every aspect of their lives and how they were going to deal with the circumstances. They took the initiative to act. Overall, they were making decisions about their Leadership Brand and Leadership Lifestyle whether they realized it or not. Leaders outside of the corporate world do the same exact thing. They find ways to lead and they do it.

Think of leadership decisions in these simple examples. If you walk by someone who needs help and you stop to help them, are you a leader compared to those who walked by and didn't help? If you stop and pick up a piece of trash on the office floor to ensure a clean work environment, you're demonstrating leading by example.

Reed Hastings, CEO of Netflix, posted some interesting slides about his company's culture and relating to trash. The title of one slide is The Rare Responsible Person, and the last bullet of that slide says: Picks up trash lying on the floor. Why? You take action. You lead by example. You take the initiative. You care.

These examples are small, and some people could debate if this demonstrates leadership ability. It does. In these examples, people made decisions that helped others or helped the community. Both are small in scale yet show the amount of initiative taken by someone. This is how we define and find value in leadership. As I mentioned earlier, I value the initiative that leaders take.

Think about it like this: Do you stop to help others? Do you hold the door or elevator for a peer coming along behind you? If yes, great. If no, why? Why couldn't, or wouldn't, you take a moment to help? Too busy? Too involved in your current tasks? Did the famous leaders that flood our minds when thinking about leadership decide not to help? Was Mother Teresa too worried about ensuring she got her Starbucks and got to a meeting on time before helping a sickly child on the corner? This is extreme to paint a picture. It shows how everything you do dictates your leadership path and how people perceive your ability to lead by your decisions.

If Mother Teresa walked down the street after warming her belly with a triple mocha, avoiding that child until later, she wouldn't have had the impact she did. Welcome to the model that will reshape your leadership mindset. Think about the last story shared about CJ and the decisions that he made. Yes, he was a leader at work and yet found other ways to lead. He made decisions. He took action. He led. Are you making decisions every day to lead? Yes or no? It's that simple.

Let's now focus on the A/P/E Model specifically and the parts of the cycle in how we make our leadership decisions. First, A stands for awareness. You need to be aware of yourself. You need to be aware of where you want and need to be. Self-awareness is the best trait leaders can demonstrate to improve their effectiveness and to become more aware of what motivates them and their decision-making. Plus, you need to be aware of the situations, surroundings, and people around you. You need to be aware of the skills and behaviors of what leaders you have, want, and need to ensure your success. You need to learn constantly.

P stands for practice. You can have all the awareness in the world about anything, but if you are looking to make a difference for yourself and those around you, you need to take action. You need to practice being a leader through your decisions daily. Not once a month. Not for the next week after reading this book. Every day. If you want to be a leader, you need to behave like a leader through taking initiative. Not tomorrow or the week after. Today. Now. You need to find ways to lead through practice. You need to look at your life and see what makes sense. You need to take an inventory and know where you can help yourself every day. The more you are willing to learn and the harder you are willing to practice, the more successful you will be at achieving your vision and goals.

Once you practice and take action to lead, you need to evaluate, which brings us to the E. Evaluation within itself can lead to awareness. The two work hand in hand within the cycle. Evaluation should help you further educate yourself about where you are within your leadership journey, what you should continue to work on, and where you're succeeding.

Evaluation encourages you to get feedback and insight based on the perceptions of others to aid in understanding your work and how it impacts others. It also asks you to self-assess as part of the cycle. Evaluation is the process for gathering and making sense of information to help you assess the success of leadership development efforts and make sound decisions about future investments. This also helps increase our awareness and fine-tune our practice.

The following chapters look more in-depth at each one of these parts of the cycle and offer suggestions on how you can begin to integrate each into your day-to-day leadership practice and decisions.

When reading, take notes whether in a journal or on your phone or your laptop. Stop and think. Take breaks. Reflect on your Leadership Brand and current situation to think about what makes sense for you now. You know better than anyone what you face, how you feel, the way you approach your day, and how you can utilize this model in your leadership decisions. You are making the decisions for you, as a leader, and for those you lead.

6

Awareness

Think about how you learn. How did you learn the alphabet? How did you learn to count? How did you learn about history? You may be shooting off answers ranging from school to teachers to parents to books to toys to the classroom to siblings to childcare to nannies to television to whatever. The list goes on and on.

Through learning, we gain awareness. Awareness matters to our brains, our growth, and our development both in our personal and professional lives. In learning, not only do we become more aware of the world by gaining knowledge, but we are also more aware of ourselves and how we fit into the world.

Leadership and learning go hand in hand. Leaders are learners. No matter where you are in your leadership journey, not only do we need to learn to adapt and grow, but we need to constantly be learning about ourselves too. Awareness is essential when thinking about the skills, traits, and behaviors when defining what makes a leader, a leader and the value that these leaders add to those they impact and influence.

In being aware, we learn. We learn about ourselves. We learn about others. We learn about what people and our business need and how we can improve and lead from this knowledge. Plus, gaining knowledge and continuous learning is a benefit to our Leadership Lifestyle. It enables us to use our awareness of how our actions had imperfect results to then adjust our actions based on the feedback in the future. This enables us to fine-tune our ability and improve our leadership effectiveness.

You will never reach the point of having to shut off your brain to learning. Its fluidity, when matched with globalization, ever-changing conditions, and leading a melting pot of generations and cultures, makes it hard to contain to one book, one course, or simply one decision. You have to be okay with including learning in your life and your leadership practice when you decide to lead. Leaders must be learners.

Through defining leadership, you're aware that leaders hold certain traits and behaviors that aid in their ability to lead. You've learned this from observing leaders, working with leaders, being a leader, and reading about leaders. In the first chapters, you defined what you know about leaders and how you specifically derive value in leadership and where there may be some misconceptions.

As a leader yourself, you are most likely aware of your strengths both at work and in life when it comes to leadership. You've gained this through feedback and life experiences. But you need to evaluate to aid in your continued success and development. You are most likely aware of some of your weaknesses too. Similarly, you need to evaluate to aid in your ongoing improvement and development. Two examples come to mind.

Kate was an emerging leader whom I worked with in various scenarios. She was hungry to advance formally within her career while broadening her business acumen. She constantly took classes and talked about how what she was learning could be applied to the business and to those above her. Not only did she talk about what she was learning, but she applied that knowledge in starting new projects to help customers. Because of those decisions, she grew as a leader and as a person. Those higher on the corporate ladder noticed her efforts and often commended her achievements both in conversation and in terms of formal promotion. Her decisions paid off.

On the other hand, Jamie was more tenured in his career and wasn't interested in developing himself. He thought he was good enough for his job and that his learning had somewhat ended due to his age and point in his career. Hey, he was going to retire in five years, so why did it matter? He said this often. Jamie's manager was concerned that Jamie's attitude about this was troublesome especially since his clients were complaining about him and his lack of support, vision, and follow-through. He wasn't trying to make things better, he wasn't interested in learning more about his client needs, and he just didn't care anymore.

Jamie's manager and I offered him several ways he could learn, develop, and grow to better aid himself and those he served. But he didn't want any of it and made the decision to keep doing what he was doing without listening to those around him. This led Jamie to lose his job since he was making better decisions about his own leadership development practice, which led to his manager thinking he didn't care enough about the job to be there anymore and that was impacting the business.

You may have been Kate or Jamie at some point or known people like Kate and Jamie. Yet, are you thinking about ways you can broaden your awareness to enhance your leadership decisions? A way to start doing this is to write a leadership story about yourself and how you acted and why. In writing, you may begin to see how certain life experiences have shaped you and your leadership decisions today. As you write, reflect on how this particular instance impacts you on a larger scale in who you are as a leader. That's one step of many.

Let's examine awareness from three standpoints:

1. The first is traditional ways of looking at formalized learning mediums along with performance management and feedback.

2. The second is gaining awareness through nontraditional ways.

3. Last, I'll introduce the idea of TOLL—or timing, opportunity, looks, and likes—and why each matter, to our leadership decisions and awareness when managing our decisions and the perceptions of those around us on how we lead.

TOLL will be included more in the practice and evaluation sections and how it drives our decisions. We will also revisit the performance management practice and feedback and introduce the idea of a Feedback Board and Success Team in the evaluation section as evaluation and awareness work hand in hand within the A/P/E Model to enhance leadership decision-making.

Traditional Approaches to Awareness

In realizing that leadership is about deciding to develop ourselves through learning and awareness followed by practice and evaluation, we can first look at the traditional approaches in gaining awareness both in the academic sense and in the corporate world. While these mediums aren't the most exciting at times, each serves a purpose in ensuring that we continue our learning as part of our Leadership Lifestyle.

Finding the time to commit to learning can be a challenge. It is essential to our leadership development. As you read, consider how you can integrate what you are learning into your Leadership Lifestyle. In the traditional sense, we'll look at formalized learning mediums followed by performance management and feedback in general. If you are a leader, you should be striving to develop knowledge to improve yourself, your company, and the people who work for you.

Formalized Learning Mediums

In thinking specifically about traditional approaches to increasing our awareness, we can turn to learning through conventional methods. I define these as reading books, articles, and research, classroom training, webinars, eLearning courses, and podcasts. Through these mediums, we can gather a level of awareness from those instructing that helps us become more aware of a particular subject matter that can enable us and inform our leadership decisions.

Awareness gives us a new perception of our circumstances, which will align with TOLL later on in this section. Plus, it builds more around the ideas that perception is reality and aligning that to our Leadership Brand and Leadership Lifestyle. Finding time to dedicate to learning is the real challenge in trying to balance our Leadership Lifestyle in incorporating learning.

Deciding on an approach that works for you is equally important. Let's look at a few in more detail. There are more options now to expand our awareness and to learn than what was available twenty, or even ten, years ago. In knowing this and in thinking about each method, consider how you can use these in your own life to enhance your awareness as part of your Leadership Lifestyle.

Reading

You've made a step in deciding your leadership by picking up this book whether you actually paid money to purchase or simply glanced out of curiosity online. That was a decision about your future. Leaders must be readers. Reading is a common way to learn. We want to learn something new when we read a book or an article. We want to understand the research.

Some hate to read or find it difficult to integrate into their lifestyle due to the time commitment. If you aren't a reader, consider audiobooks or skip ahead to learn more about using webinars, eLearning, and podcasts. If you do prefer to read a book, article, or research to learn, let's look at the benefits further. We know that reading is vital to keep our brains active and healthy. Reading is also the way we can learn something new and then apply that information to both our life and leadership.

There are plenty of books on leadership. Many are very good. On the one hand, this is incredibly helpful as we can find numerous texts that could make a difference in the way that we view and become leaders. On the other hand, it can be overwhelming with so many options to consider.

In knowing that we'd have enough on our reading list to fill up an entire lifetime, it's important to assess what you think is most important to you and your leadership journey. Maybe this book is your first attempt. Alternatively, perhaps it's your fifth or even hundredth. If you consider expanding your awareness from books and aren't sure where to start, the best way is to reflect on your definition of what makes a leader, a leader. Consider, too, if you wrote down a name of someone you know or could gain access to when defining leadership. Ask that person what the last leadership book they read was and that can start you on your reading path.

Later on, we'll look in more detail at creating a Success Team and a Feedback Board to expand our awareness and to gain evaluation. These people also could provide recommendations. Along with reading books, another way to gain awareness is through articles. Magazines, newspapers, and the internet are filled with articles and commentary on leadership. This is the quicker way to think about integrating current information into our schedules and during our day. These can also be more present to what's happening here and now compared to that of a book, so the timeliness helps.

In following a similar approach as suggested with books, turning to those you admire for recommendations on resources to check out can be your first step. Or you could venture on your own in your search. If you prefer the academic route, you can also seek journals and research to further your awareness and to guide your decisions. Venturing down this path in enhancing your understanding can be daunting due to the level of material depending on where you are in your level of understanding.

Regardless of what you read, find content that interests you that you can use in your own life. Find and dedicate the time to do so. I've found myself struggling with reading some leadership books. Some overcomplicate leadership while some oversimplify. If you start something and don't like it, decide to stop reading. Stick with content that you find useful.

Find material that will add value to your life. Find content that you want to read. That will make the difference in helping you stay motivated. Later on, in helping to expand your level of awareness, in Part III, we will focus specifically on skills and behaviors you can consider in developing your leadership capacity and enhancing your leadership decisions.

Classroom Training

Taking a course can be another way to expand your level of awareness about leadership. It can also be a venue for you to meet people to build your network and to find people to incorporate into your Feedback Board and Success Team.

In taking leadership courses, you can look to complete your knowledge in various ways.

Sure, we can take a class at the local college or university. Or maybe we have a local community education program where we can learn. Classroom-based courses can give us the discipline we may need to focus on learning in having someone tell us what to read, what to respond to, and what to provide our analysis on via research papers and presentations. Depending on your level of interest in moving forward with leadership, several colleges and universities offer formalized degrees. Remember the example in the introduction to this book when I asked, What do you plan to study in school? and being surprised to hear leadership.

In seeing the demand for leadership education, it is of no surprise that the academic world is creating degrees that meet this need. Not only does the academic world see this, but the corporate world does as well. Maybe you work for an organization that offers formal leadership training. If you do, this can be a way to gain this training as part of your formalized career role and development.

When needing help to develop executives and their leadership abilities, some organizations will turn to universities to complete such a task. Corporate education programs provide executives with the academic component in conjunction with the practical application to the business. These programs include various forms of learning from lectures to team building assignments to role plays.

One component of these programs is being able to receive feedback about yourself from your peers. Feedback aids in awareness. Feedback and evaluation are critical in helping us make well-informed decisions about our leadership. Asking for feedback can give leaders insight into their blind spots, ensuring greater self-awareness and a deeper understanding of how they need to improve their performance.

More considerations: Beth is a sales vice president at an organization and is focused on customer success. She and the rest of the executive team take a three-day leadership program at a local university. During the duration of the course, she has to define her value to give feedback to her peers and to listen to her peers give her feedback on how they perceive her as a leader.

Being a to-do list addict as a task-orientated person, she knows this about herself and her brand. Beth's peers also define her as someone they can count on to "get stuff done" and share that feedback with her during the course. With her level of drive and motivation for managing customer success for people using the products, you'd want to have someone who's motivated and driven to get things done and done quickly.

We need to be aware of skills, behaviors, circumstances, and traits and how others perceive us, which we can learn through hearing feedback. Utilizing classroom-based training whether on our own or through work can be a way to enable us to expand this level of awareness about leadership to make further improvements to our Leadership Lifestyle and decisions.

Webinars, eLearning, and Podcasts

Although webinars, eLearning, and podcasts are a bit newer to the realm of learning, I consider these to be more traditional than not. Webinars, eLearning, and podcasts enhance the mobility of learning and can also attract those who may not have the time or patience to sit through a class or read a book. These mediums make learning so easy.

Have a commute? Find an interesting podcast or webinar to listen to during that time. Like lectures and engaging content? Take an eLearning course through a site like Coursera or LinkedIn Learning during your lunch break.

In thinking about the mobility of learning, we can learn anywhere at any time. We can download apps to our phones that make it easy enough to access at the touch of a finger. The beauty of these mediums is that they are immediate in thinking about the relevancy of content. Books and articles can take years to reach their readers. Classroom instructors could be using content that's dated. These broadcasts are happening all the time and are happening right now, and the learning is up-to-date and can be applicable that day.

What's helpful about these options, too, and this depends on your situation in both life and career, is that many of these options are free. With the other options that we've looked at, there's a cost associated. Classes cost money. Books cost money. However, online learning is mostly free. What makes these options so amazing is that they are open to anyone. Why? Because anyone can learn to lead.

Leadership isn't only for the select few who have the resources to spend to get the best degrees or buy the best books. It's for everyone. Everyone can learn and expand their awareness to be a leader. The only investment is time. You can find the time. You need to decide to do so. Consider how you can integrate learning into your own life.

Performance Management

Awareness can also come via the work-based performance management review where you hear an appraisal from your manager about your performance over the past year.

To define:

▸ Performance management is the process of identifying, measuring, managing, and developing the performance of human resources in an organization.

▸ Performance appraisal is the ongoing process of evaluating employee performance.

During this process, you hear from your manager on what you've done well, or not so well, throughout the year. The performance review, both the evaluation and meeting, may encompass feedback from your peers, clients, and organizational leaders. Here you can gain awareness through evaluation and feedback concerning your job and in growing yourself as a leader.

I add performance management here when thinking about awareness, but will outline further when we examine evaluation as part of the A/P/E Model. Performance management reviews are evaluations of the work and performance against your job and organizational goals and objectives. Remember, though, that these are solely job-role based. You can have that job today, but you may not have it tomorrow.

We need to remember that we can only trust jobs, employers, and bosses to help with our self-awareness and leadership development and only to an extent. If you want to lead, you need to make that decision for yourself. This doesn't come from a manager telling you to lead during your performance management review. It's your decision and a part of your lifestyle.

It's an essential medium to gain awareness about yourself and behavior that you may not have had insight into before especially in thinking of formalized leadership roles within organizations. Many employees dread performance reviews. Many dread the idea of feedback. Why? Because it's scary to hear that the work we do each day may not be valued or appreciated. We may not be good enough, and that can hurt our ego.

In knowing that, and even having that level of awareness about how we approach feedback, we can reframe this practice and how we internalize what we hear. We can approach with fear and a closed mind, or we can approach as a learning opportunity to help us hear what we need to work on to further build ourselves as leaders. Remember to frame this work-based practice in a way that will be helpful to you as it can be of value if done and approached right.

Feedback

In building on performance management, the word *feedback* can strike fear in the hearts of those being told, "I've got some feedback for you." Panic sets in. Why? Wouldn't this be exciting? Why can't this be seen as an opportunity? Effective and timely feedback is a critical component of a successful performance management program and should be used in conjunction with setting performance goals.

Somehow, we've been programmed to fear feedback. When we usually hear the word, it's used about something we've screwed up that we need to fix in moving forward from our manager. Many, not all, don't hear feedback and think that something positive is on its way based on our past encounters. It's sad. That within itself should be something we push to change as leaders and to learn to embrace as part of our growth.

We need to reframe the way we look at feedback—from something to dread associated with a power difference to that of opportunity and something we share with everyone freely. The easiest yet hardest thing we can do to get feedback to aid in our awareness is to ask those around us. We also need to think about how we give feedback as many of us suck at it.

Ask questions like this:

- What am I doing well as a leader?

- What could I improve?

- What would you like to see more of from me over the next _____ (time frame)?

- What's one thing that you see holding me back?

- What's a success of mine that you've seen?

Questions like this open dialogue to discuss perceptions and realities. We become aware of people's perceptions of us. Feedback and feedback-related training is the rage in the corporate development world with the push being moving from traditional performance management reviews to that of more open and honest feedback given on a regular basis.

The way we can gain awareness at work about our leadership ability is through feedback. As mentioned earlier we see this with the annual performance management cycle. In opening arms and reframing the way that we feel about feedback, we can begin to embrace it. In making that decision, we can start to hear what people are telling us based on their perceptions of our behavior and how it relates to us as leaders.

In having that data, we can put the A/P/E Model into use. We've gained the awareness through the feedback and then can move on to practice and then evaluate all over again. The pain in this is toughening our skin enough not only to accept feedback but also to gain comfort in asking for it on a regular basis if you aren't already.

That within itself can further position us as leaders as people then hear and see our dedication to improving our leadership practice. That's an important decision to make. Think to yourself again: Feedback is an opportunity for awareness. Feedback broadens our awareness and helps us make better decisions. But we also have to consider the source of feedback and whether or not it will be useful to us in our leadership overall.

These traditional approaches are practical and helpful in gaining more understanding about leadership skills and behaviors. In Part III, we will look at evaluation regarding skills and will look at common leadership behaviors that we can build through our decisions and through using the A/P/E Model. The traditional approaches to learning can only take you so far, in any case. These are broad strokes on the canvas of leadership. They aren't personal to you. You're the one you care about developing and improving.

Nontraditional Approaches to Awareness

After reading the books, listening to the podcasts, watching the online courses, hearing the feedback, and taking the classes, you'll

▸ Be worn out, and

▸ Wonder what you are going to do to make a change that will impact your own life.

Let's address ways you can pivot on these traditional mediums and get creative in thinking about other ways you can gain awareness. I call these nontraditional as they mix some traditional ways with a new way of thinking. Some of these approaches may be easier to do, whereas some may be a stretch in considering your level of comfort with being forthcoming about your leadership practice and indeed taking charge on how you expand your level of awareness.

Self-Surveys

Some people are scared to tell the truth or share their perceptions and opinions when thinking about giving feedback especially in using work-based feedback tools. If you can find straightforward people who can give you feedback to expand your awareness specifically about your leadership ability, then you'll benefit immensely. For the sake of talking about survey, let's assume that you feel that people on your teams or in your life are holding back from being honest with you when it comes to your leadership ability.

This is more often the case than not. In reflecting on traditional approaches, we talked about feedback and performance management and a thread within that being able to receive feedback at work if your organization integrates this into their practice. Maybe they do, but perhaps they don't. Relying on the standard performance management cycle at work can be superficial as it only provides one view of who you are as a leader.

You can only trust the organization where you are employed to help with your development to a certain extent. The rest is up to you if you are genuinely dedicated to making a change in your behavior to enhance your leadership. In knowing that leadership is a lifestyle, we should look for feedback both in our formal roles at work and also include the feedback from those who experience our leadership outside of work.

To gain awareness through feedback, you can turn to surveys to learn how others perceive and experience your leadership. You can take advantage of survey tools like Survey Monkey to survey those around you on your ability and development at work, in the community, and in your personal life.

Using a tool like this, you can gain feedback anonymously. It will not only help you receive the feedback and awareness that you need to make decisions but could also help in avoiding hurt feelings and damaged relationships. Why does that matter? Feedback can be hard to take. Depending on whom we ask, we may take some messages easier than others from certain people and in considering the relationship.

Within this medium, you have the flexibility to ask whatever you want to whomever you want to hear feedback from. Whose perceptions matter to you? Why? In gaining awareness through feedback, you may also want to consider a time line of what makes sense. You could ask three questions about development every three months. Or one question monthly for a year.

Sample questions could include these:

▸ What, if anything, have you noticed me do differently in (this area)? What else would you suggest I do differently?

▸ What are you seeing me do well as a leader?

▸ Where could I continue to improve?

> ▶ What would you want to see more from me in the way that I lead?

> ▶ What other feedback can you provide to me that would further aid in my development?

In fashioning these questions, you can begin to form this survey that will be instrumental to your path and your decisions. You don't want to inundate those around with your surveys weekly or daily as change can take time to happen and be noticed. Keeping to a quarterly or biannual schedule may help you truly work on behavior change and not overwhelm those from whom you seek feedback. You need to tell people you are working on the behavior and changing yourself, so they know to look out for those changes. Keeping this process a secret benefits no one. That's how you can get people on board in your journey and invite them to provide you with awareness through feedback.

In a training I conducted, a man around my age gave me feedback after the session. He said he felt like he couldn't connect with me. I sounded too corporate, too HR. He felt that tone lessened his learning and his overall experience with me. I looked at that as a challenge. I decided I'd try and be more like my whole "Catherine" persona and began opening up more over the years in future trainings. I never received that feedback through any sort of formality but through someone who was willing to be open and honest with me to truly make an impact.

People seemed more open to me once I started being honest about applying the training content to work and the related challenges. My relationships with those I trained got better once I started to be more open, more honest, and more me. Years later, that same man was in my class. I asked if the training was better in how he experienced me and what he learned. He gave me a thumbs-up. That feedback meant the world to me, and I was able to make a real change to how I led training courses and connected with people on the topic of leadership.

Informational Interviewing

Informational interviewing is a fancy phrase. It's a way that we take a straightforward idea and make it seem corporate-worthy and academically and cocktail party enticing. That word is *talking*. Moreover, specifically, talking to other people. Talking is a lost art. With social media, texts, discussion boards, and online meetings, we've forgotten how to speak and to hear from people in a way that can help us grow. Talking helps us create and foster our relationships. Finding the time to stop, to have these conversations, to listen, and to nurture can go a long way for us as a leader and for our relationships.

Taking the time to talk to those around us provides perspective and gives us the awareness that we need to make better, more informed decisions about ourselves as leaders and those we impact. That gives us more awareness.

Talking to people overall gives us more insight. It also helps to change the perspective that those around us may have.

I once was doing workshops on collaboration across an organization. As part of the pre-work, the participants were assigned to talk to someone else within the organization. For about an hour, they needed to get to know that person on a personal level while also learning about their role within the organization. It was merely relationship-building work.

Relationships are the foundation for collaboration. Healthy relationships with people ensure that things get done. In asking some of these participants to talk to others, it was as if I had asked them to commit a felony. I'm being that extreme as some were horrified that they had to talk to someone. Some expressed that openly. Some weren't as vocal and didn't make the time.

Many people did complete the assignment and guess what they said? They said they got to know someone and, from getting to know that person, felt like their relationship was further forming, being repaired, or created.

In one of the first workshops I taught, I asked the executive who was sponsoring it if there were any troublemakers in the class that I should watch out for. He noted that a director named Thom might cause some issues.

Thom wasn't getting along with his boss and was challenging this executive and others in a less than helpful fashion, so people were feeling frustrated and annoyed with him. The day of the workshop, I saw where Thom was sitting and made a mental note to keep an eye on him. In asking the class what their reactions from the pre-work were, Thom raised his hand. My heart skipped a beat. This was it. After being quiet all morning, he was going to have his go at me.

These situations can be some of the worst parts of doing leadership training—waiting for someone to rip into me for their political reasons and agenda within an organization. It can be somewhat exciting, too, as people can surprise you with what comes out of their mouth. He began, "I was hesitant about this." Of course. And continued, "I got much value out of doing this. I talked to someone whom I work with often, but didn't know."

He went on as I exhaled in relief, "In sitting down and talking to Ralph, I learned a lot about what he does in the sales division and how it impacts what I do. It was a perfect conversation, and it will do a lot for our relationship in the way that we move forward."

I was thrilled. Ralph, his talking partner, then raised his hand and supported Thom's remarks. His words were perfect at the moment. What did this exercise in talking to someone give Thom? It gave him the awareness that he didn't have before talking to Ralph. Something as simple as that—having a short conversation with a person—gave him so much awareness that he would have never had before being assigned this exercise.

To lead, we need to talk along with asking good questions and then listen to the answers. Whether you're an introvert or extrovert, we need to speak to those around us. We can do that by talking to others to both gain perspective and viewpoints but also to figure out what and how that person can enhance our awareness. We can look to people at work, like bosses and VPs and coworkers, but we can also expand that to talk to our family, our friends, and others we come in contact with whether it be at work or in our personal lives.

If leadership touches both professional and personal parts of our life, making it a lifestyle, we need to be asking everyone around us for perspective, feedback, and knowledge. We need to talk and listen to learn. We can talk to our peers, our friends, and our family. We can speak with our organizational leadership. We can speak with our community leaders. We can attend events and meet new people to talk with. We can take classes and work with people to talk with. Talking gives us awareness. We may forget that, but it's how we can expand our networks and enhance our awareness by the perceptions of those we speak with.

7

Awareness in Timing, Opportunity, Looks, and Likes (TOLL)

Now that we've addressed ways to increase your awareness as part of the A/P/E Model and this element of the cycle, let's add a level of realness to help you examine your own life and find ways to take initiative. In looking at life, and then thinking specifically about leadership, let's focus on the fundamentals of TOLL to perceptions and awareness. TOLL stands for timing, opportunity, looks, and likes. See what I mean? Scientific.

TOLL includes a layer of awareness that other leadership books do not address. Some of these elements may seem like common career knowledge or knowledge that many of us overlook. Maybe we haven't adequately addressed these elements in thinking about our lives and our leadership practice. However, we should. Some of this may seem superficial in some ways yet pose common barriers to advancing in leadership whether we want to admit it or not.

We can do everything right in our own lives; we can make the right decisions and treat people well. Yet, things still may not happen to us: love, promotions, and money, for example. It can be frustrating when we feel like we're doing everything right yet can't progress in our lives. Agonizing even. It's important to give these elements thought when we think about our lives and leadership and how we use our decisions to move forward as leaders.

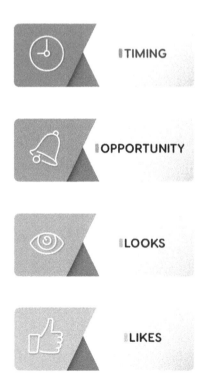

Let me break down each element and then apply it to leadership and how we make decisions about our growth and development along with aligning to our Leadership Brand and Leadership Lifestyle. In having TOLL for consideration as part of the A/P/E Model, we can further expand our level of awareness about our situations, our lifestyles, and our path forward with our decisions.

Timing

Notice how some things in life seems to happen at the right time? Or the wrong time? Our lives revolve around time. Timing is everything. Timing, when we think about leadership, is everything too. Consider these aspects when it comes to timing and leadership:

▸ How we manage our time to practice

▸ How we use our time to find opportunity

We judge ourselves on how we manage time. We judge leaders on how they operate and use time too. We also look at time in other ways when it comes to leadership in thinking about the formality of a promotion, which can take time. Or, one day, it could fall in our lap with a change in the organization or from a call from a recruiter with a new offer or a friend detailing a unique opportunity with a start-up. Timing, and using it to our advantage in changing our behavior, matters immensely when establishing ourselves as leaders. We know that we can't control time, but we can control our decisions around how we use it. We can't control timing, but we can find ways to take advantage of it to our benefit.

I once heard a CEO support the idea of timing and using it to one's benefit. It was simple in that it came down to outworking someone else to make time work to your advantage. People often complain about how quickly time passes. Alternatively, how there doesn't seem to be enough time in the day. Time seems to take up more time in conversations than we may even want to admit. We can look at time as an enemy. Or we can look at time as a friend that we are looking to manage better. That's what it comes down to: finding ways to manage time to our benefit and making a decision to. Each day we have the opportunity to make time to improve our lives, our careers, and our leadership through our decisions.

I think about my time a lot and how I can make the most impact during the day. I make lists from day to day and year to year and consider each day how I can make progress toward achieving what's on my lists. I frame this as, "Where can I make decisions (whether large or small) that will help me practice my leadership and influence?" From my answers to those questions, I can decide where it makes the most sense for me to take initiative to act.

Think about your to-do list. Maybe there's one thing on there that you always put off doing day after day, week after week. Where can you reframe your decisions about time management to become more effective?

People tend to put off decisions about their development and their leadership. They wait until the "right time" or they "wait until they have the time" and it passes and they never progress forward. They wait for the promotions thinking that this will grant leadership when the time is right and it doesn't. I attended an event once where the young woman who started up an app for pharmaceuticals talked about the difference between men and women when it comes to business and leadership. She mentioned that women wait. They wait until the right time to lead. They wait until they've checked all the boxes. We all need to make decisions to act. We can't wait. Time ticks by.

It's also the mindset of not only finding the time, but finding the time to create our own opportunity whether the time is right or not. If an opportunity to lead a project or to step up in the community comes our way, take that step. It's a step to practice. Opportunity can appear in ways that we least expect like our manager saying we aren't ready for a promotion. In an example like this, we can stay at the organization and continue to work hard hoping that this perception changes or make the decision to leave to maximize our time somewhere else.

Each day, we all have the same hours to work with. Some use them better than others. Learning how to use those days, hours, and minutes to our advantage as leaders can be a challenge and a challenge we need to master to lead. People waste time on Facebook. People waste time on gossiping. People waste time in various ways. People make decisions to waste time. People can decide to stop wasting time, too, and make time to focus on how they will use their decisions to advance.

Sometimes, even if we manage time right and to our advantage, opportunities present themselves and the timing isn't right no matter how excellent the opportunity. Sometimes we have to say no to the opportunity offered at the wrong time. As leaders, we need to know when to say no and take care of ourselves when we have feelings of stress or frustration. Sometimes the timing is right, and that's when we need to decide to say yes to that timing even if we're scared, timid, or have self-doubt.

Think about the timing of your life. Now think about what else you want to do for the rest of your life. You only have so much of it. How are you going to make decisions about it now that will impact your leadership today and into the future? It's also important to remember that it takes time to change perceptions. It takes time to change our behavior.

On average, it takes more than two months before a new behavior becomes automatic—66 days to be exact. The time it takes a new habit to form can vary widely depending on the behavior, the person, and the circumstances, ranging anywhere from 18 days to 254 days. In knowing that, how can you make better decisions about how to use timing to your benefit and your Leadership Lifestyle? Timing ties into the next aspect of this: opportunity.

Opportunity comes at the right time, or the wrong time. It's different from the way that we manage time during our day making it essential to understand the similarities and the differences.

Opportunity

Opportunity is essential when it comes to leadership. Opportunity opens doors whether we create it for ourselves or seize it when we see it. We can look at the opportunity in two ways:

▶ How we decide to react and seize opportunities that come to us

▶ How we decide to seek and create opportunities for ourselves

As leaders, we can make decisions to create opportunities for ourselves and take initiative when we see that things need to be done whether at work or in the community. Sometimes opportunity finds us through a connection we made at a networking event or in a class. Opportunity can come to us at various points and at various times. Yet, our decisions dictate how we benefit as leaders from these opportunities whatever they may be.

If opportunity—and call this what you will (job promotion, lead on a project, chance to head up a community group, or create something with a friend)—happens at a good time, then we must decide to use it to our advantage and make that decision and not be afraid. Right timing varies from person to person, but we all have a grasp on what we can handle at different points in our life. Taking advantage of this can lead us down a path.

It can give us this time to take advantage of an opportunity to enhance our leadership ability and further practice and make decisions. Opportunity can present itself at difficult times. Whether it is due to family or other life circumstances, at times, we may need to decline. Sometimes we need to say no. When we do this, as leaders, we are trying to make the best decision for ourselves during that period. Saying yes could lead us down a path where we aren't able to make our best leadership decisions, and that could impact us more than saying no.

Think about it like this: If you get a new project at work and have a busy family calendar and someone asks you to partner on a side project, you may need to give thought to this commitment. It could damage your impact at work, and time at home may lessen because you're being stretched to a point where your Leadership Lifestyle is compromised. We should be seeking opportunities. No one tells a leader to lead; we decide to do this or not.

At work, we can ask for more opportunity to lead. We can do this by asking to lead projects or initiatives. We can talk to leaders and those in our community. We can explore areas that piggyback on or create opportunities for ourselves.

Situations like these are when we have to decide on how can we create our opportunities to lead. Leadership isn't merely a title or a given, just because someone tells us to lead. We need to make this decision for ourselves. We need to know when we need to create our opportunity. You can do this in various ways. Maybe it comes in starting a group at work. Perhaps it comes from a side project that you've wanted to work on further. Maybe you aren't quite sure and, from being aware of this, can take a step back as the idea will come when it may and can give you your opportunity. Sometimes, to lead and find ways to practice our leadership behaviors, we need to decide to create opportunities for ourselves to lead and to say yes when the timing is right when opportunities are offered to us.

In thinking back to the story of Jacob and the pedicab, Nathan created an opportunity for Jacob to lead. I also think of other leaders whom I've worked with who have led formally within the corporate world, but made time to volunteer or start side ventures to lead in other aspects of their life. We all have the chance to lead whether it be at work or at home. We simply need to think about what those opportunities are for us and how we can make decisions to use them to our advantage.

Looks

As I described at the beginning of this chapter, some of what TOLL outlines can seem superficial especially when it comes to how people look. The concept of looks was something that we challenged with our leadership definition in considering bias and misconceptions. Yet, it's one that I hear talked about behind closed doors when others judge us based on first impressions and biased mindsets. It's also one that I've struggled with in being taught in school that "it's what's on the inside that counts." In this section, I ask you to consider the following:

▶ How and if appearance is impacting the perceptions of you (fairly or unfairly) as they relate to their perception of your leadership (maybe you care, maybe you don't)

▶ How you feel as a leader in the way that you think you "look" to others in managing perceptions

This story pains me, but it is one that, sadly, makes a point within the corporate world. Carolyn reports to a woman named Tanya. Carolyn is short, dark, and heavyset and wears simple clothing. Tanya is blond, tall, thin, and well-dressed. Tanya was promoted almost every year within the organization, and Carolyn has been there about two years without any sort of movement. Carolyn wanted to be promoted and eventually to become a leader in a formal sense within the company.

One day I was meeting with a colleague, Carl, who during our conversation began talking about the two women. Carl was tall, thin, and very well-dressed. He made a comment that Tanya, although a leader within the organization, wasn't that bright. Tanya had been there "in a pinch" when things needed to get done, hence got promoted.

He also felt another factor was that Tanya was in better shape along with being attractive and well-dressed. Carl noted, "She looks like a leader." Carl talked further about how Carolyn was dowdy and overweight, which would hinder a formal promotion within the organization even though she was far more intelligent and more of a natural leader than Tanya. Carolyn's looks, not her brains and ability, would hold her back, unlike the physical attributes of her manager. I wanted to scream and cry at how unfair this was, but I sat there quietly and nodded.

We know that life is not fair and people judge on looks. These are the conversations that people have about others when defining leadership and who looks the part and can walk the walk. Think about this: The typical chief executive is more than six feet tall, has a deep voice, a good posture, a touch of gray in his thick, lustrous hair, and, for his age, a fit body. Those around him will think, "Hey, he looks the part. He must be a leader." It also reflects earlier points about bias and our friend the forty-something, White male VP and how we use him when we define leadership. These observations happen when people have conversations about promotions and leadership in the formal sense.

Maybe it matters to some more than others. Maybe not. And it's not to say that you need to be attractive to lead. But it is a bias that some have, albeit superficial and maddening. Some theories like Great Man Theory and Trait Theory support the point that either you are born a leader or not. These theories also state that leaders are born with certain traits and characteristics, even including physical appearances, which determine a person's leadership success. Bias creeps in too.

I felt this firsthand when I was meeting with a manager of mine. I had gained some weight. This person kept talking to me how I needed balance in my life and eyed me up and down. Furthermore, I was told that only "pretty and thin" people would be promoted and those who dressed well. So I made the decision to lose the weight and look at my lifestyle. I bought better clothes and thought this would pay off. It didn't. I never got promoted. My confidence as a leader and as a person dwindled. I didn't even like myself as I felt like I didn't look the part based on someone else's definition of what leadership is when it comes to looks.

There's a particular rage that comes when talking about looks and leadership. Even with the story earlier about Hillary and Mark when my look of being tired was mistaken for boredom—that's what was perceived and then being judged on. The other leadership books don't talk about this and how the way you look impacts your leadership. Does this matter? You may answer yes. You may answer no. You may hesitate in answering as you know there's a level of truth in this and have been in these types of conversations before.

Maybe many of us already know this and are okay with it one way or another in defining our leadership in how we look. Maybe it stings some when reading that our promotions are dependent on whether or not people like the way we look. We can make decisions to give thought to the looks of those around us. Or not. Maybe we can simply agree that this is superficial and make the decision to broaden our own awareness.

We can define the idea of looks in thinking about others in this way:

- Our physical appearance and how those around us judge that in determining our leadership ability and the leadership ability of others

- How people perceive the way we look, or behave, in settings where we can, or do not, assert our leadership ability

In understanding, we can make decisions about the physical aspects alongside the perception aspects. People make superficial first impressions when they don't know us or who we are. We can't control this. We also still need to be true to ourselves in who we are through how we dress, how we behave, and how this, ultimately, impacts who we are as leaders and our Leadership Brand.

Likes

As you read this section, keep this in mind:

- You need to like yourself as a person and as a leader.

- You may want to consider if those around you like you in a way that's going to be beneficial to your growth and leadership development both from a personal sense and a career sense.

As I was sitting in an office one afternoon, my manager, Suzanne, sat across from me and told me that people don't like me. Honestly, she was the one who didn't like me. I'd known that all along. I sat there stunned and horrified, though, that she could even say this to me. I had asked about promotion before this talk began. She laughed. She wasn't going to promote me. I had reported to this woman off and on for several years and knew she didn't like me. She was quite vocal about her feelings toward me both in this moment and to others over the years.

Before reporting to Suzanne for the third time, I was reporting to another woman, Tess, who told me I was ready for a promotion, yet this woman left before it happened. I had been excited to grow more as a leader within that formality. Now, here we were, debating whether or not I was liked enough by Suzanne, which I was not, and the impact this would have on any promotion.

Suzanne attacked every part of who I was as a person. She did not like me. She was never going to promote me. Everything I did was wrong. Over time, I had begun not to like my job and those I worked with. I also began not to like myself as I let this woman's comments over the years impact my perceptions of myself. Working under this toxic and destructive person hurt me to my core. I began drinking more, crying often, and doubting who I was as a person and as a leader. She eventually fired me, and I couldn't fight back anymore.

A few months later, I was at a new company where I was flourishing. My new manager told me that I was liked and was on track for a promotion because of how easily I connected with others. He told me that people trusted me. People found value in me. People wanted to work with me. Even though I could see and feel this happening, I felt like a fraud since the last manager had attacked me viciously over the years in ruining my self-esteem as a leader and as a person.

Whose perceptions were right about me and whose were wrong? Like I said earlier on, perception is reality, which impacts us as leaders about our decisions and lifestyle more than we might think.

People are promoted on whether they are liked or not by those making that decision. We define good leaders by those we like and those we don't. We define leaders on how they look, or how we perceive them based on how they look. Studies prove it. Think back to our example of looks when it came to Tanya and Carolyn. Tanya was liked and promoted because of her looks. Her manager liked her. She was promoted. Tanya wasn't crazy about Carolyn. I've seen phenomenal leaders let go from organizations because they fought with the CEO or those who socialized after hours with their manager get promoted year after year.

You may have been in similar circumstances or seen it happen around you. We see people who are terrible leaders get promoted because they are liked by upper management.

They play the game. We see people who are hard workers and smart not being promoted as someone doesn't see the value that they add and doesn't particularly like them. Is that fair? No. Does it happen? Yes. All the time.

We need to look at this through a few separate lenses. First, we need to like those we surround ourselves with at work, at home, or in other ways we lead. If we don't like the people we are around, and those around us don't like us, we are never going to be useful as leaders.

Second, you need to like yourself. Who are you? What do you like about yourself? That may sound like a fourth-grade essay question, but if you don't like yourself, how can you invest the time and resources in yourself to aid in your leadership development and decisions especially if you are around people who don't support you?

It's not about being popular or straying from your brand and your values. It is about considering where there are people in your life who may block you because of their own biases toward you. It's even going as far as wondering if these biases are hurting you in ways that you may not even know. It's also a matter of considering how you like yourself and where there may be further opportunity to grow and accept yourself in order to lead and influence along with feeling confident in your ability to take initiative.

In understanding TOLL (timing, opportunity, looks, and likes), we can clarify our realities and how we can make better decisions in understanding how each element works together. This, along with the other methods of awareness discussed, can help us broaden our knowledge and make better-informed decisions on what to practice through our leadership decisions. As we move into the next chapter, we will further examine our leadership decisions concerning the A/P/E Model and TOLL.

8

Practice

Imagine that one afternoon you are sitting in a conference room listening to the senior vice president (SVP) of marketing and products practice his speech for an upcoming user group meeting composed of over 5,000 of your organization's top customers. This speech is important. It sets the foundation for the entire event and is essential for establishing the vision for the year. Your peers surround you along with several vice presidents. These people are the masterminds behind the speech.

As the SVP presents, you sit there, and after scanning the room to gauge the reactions of others, you think to yourself, "This speech is awful!" After thinking that, you wonder why everyone else is sitting there smiling and nodding as if it's okay. After concluding, he asks for feedback. This request is met with positive comments from those in the room. You're stunned. This speech will ruin the meeting. You know it. This speech will destroy the marketing of your organization's products. This speech could ruin the company.

Now you have a decision. Do you constructively provide your feedback to help this SVP deliver something that's meaningful? Or say nothing?

In doing this, you risk making those above you look bad and also risk damaging the relationship you have with the SVP and endangering your job. Do you let the speech be delivered as is and thus align yourself with those nodding faces around you assuring him of its value and then let them, as well as you, suffer the repercussions after it's delivered?

You take a day to think it over. You decide to tell him and schedule a quick meeting to give him your feedback. The day comes where the two of you are scheduled to meet. You're nervous walking into the office but know you are doing the right thing for him and the company. After you provide feedback and possible points for inclusion, he sits back and thinks for a moment. Your heart beats faster as you doubt your decision. His mouth opens.

"Thank you," he begins as you assume this will now be followed by, "I'll take this as your termination notice." He doesn't say those things.

"Thank you. I thought this sounded off. Everyone kept telling me it was fine. I didn't believe it, but couldn't get feedback that would help improve it," he says instead.

Over the next few days, you meet with him to talk about your ideas for improvements and suggestions. The speech makes a turn for the better, and he thanks you for your honest feedback and your decision to share it. It was a hard decision to make. It was a risk. In this particular case, all worked out. Who was the leader in this? Those with titles saw no issue with the speech. They said nothing. Did they realize how bad it was?

If they did, why weren't they willing to vocalize? Fear? Greed? Someone with a lower title in the hierarchy (you) stepped up to leadership in this scenario. It's a situation like this that can make or break your career and your leadership. Here we see that leaders are not titles.

Titles dictate functions, roles, and responsibilities within jobs. Jobs that you can have today, but could be gone tomorrow. This type of situation dictates your leadership practice through your decisions and the impact that your decisions can make not only for yourself but for those around you and your organization. Sometimes we need to decide to take a risk and see how things play out. That's a decision within itself and a moment of truth.

Situations like this can happen at any point in life—work, home, social life, community activity. We sometimes sit back and wait for others to speak up, to take action, to give the feedback and make the decisions. That is not leadership. Leadership is deciding to act, to practice. In this case, you chose to speak up and take action. We can't follow people who don't act. This is why so much of my own definition of leadership is rooted in initiative.

Are you finding ways to do this in your day to help position yourself as a leader? Are you one of those people merely happy with the title and compensation without taking action? Maybe you don't take action due to fear. We can let fear dictate our decisions, or lack thereof, and be complacent. Or we can decide to lead, and that's what separates leaders from those directly in roles as part of organizational functions.

In this situation, you practiced being a leader by deciding to act and speak up, and thereby you were a leader. Why does that matter? Well, practice makes perfect. Practice makes perfect. Practice makes perfect. What does that mean? Well, nothing. There's no such thing as perfect. Ever. Especially when it comes to leadership.

Leadership is messy; let's face it. Leadership is organizing people in complicated work situations to complete projects. Leadership is heading up an association. Leadership is gathering people toward a cause each week. What it comes down to is that leadership is how we define it and the behaviors and ideas of those who see us as leaders and what we do. If we want to be leaders, we need to practice leadership through our decisions every day that relate to our brand, our lifestyle, and our story. That's what makes leadership a lifestyle and not simply a job role or title. It takes practice. Practice, like anything, is easier said than done. We get distracted. We get off track. We get frustrated.

Whether it be learning how to drive, needlepoint, or cook, learning and practicing something new can be difficult.

Mastering a habit can be difficult and can take time. Taking the time to dedicate to practicing something new and hard can also be difficult. Think about your habits and if you've ever tried to break a bad habit whether it was biting your nails or quitting smoking, it doesn't happen overnight. It takes time to break habits, to develop new ones, and to change behavior.

Being a leader and practicing leadership behaviors isn't something we can change at the snap of a finger. It's something we need to commit to and make a decision to do just that. This aligns itself with TOLL (timing, opportunity, looks, and likes) in specifically thinking about timing and opportunity. When thinking about both these elements of TOLL, we need to make the time to practice. We need to find and create the opportunity to do so.

Without making the decision to incorporate this into our lifestyle and finding ways to practice, the message in this book, along with anything else we do to increase our awareness, is lost. There are many ways in which we can practice our leadership. In this chapter, we will examine practicing leadership from three different viewpoints that also align to opportunity and initiative:

▶ How can we practice at work and in the typical job sense?

▶ How can we practice outside of work in how we further develop our ability?

With each, we will incorporate aspects of TOLL and awareness in considering the A/P/E Model. In doing so, it will help you frame your decisions in moving forward on your leadership path. Throughout, you should consider your circumstances and how you can do this regularly and make decisions to do so while seeking new opportunities to practice and to be a leader.

On the Job

When we define leadership, we think of people. We think of people who are politicians, activists, and religious figureheads. We also think of the people we work with. We know these people. We interact with these people. We know that these leaders are attainable in our day-to-day. So, naturally, these people also come to mind when asked. At work, and keeping in mind the O of TOLL when thinking about the opportunity, it can be the most comfortable place to begin our practice. We can ask for projects. We can lead initiatives. We can find ways to practice our leadership if we work in a supportive environment to do so.

Let's look at a few ways you can practice and enhance your leadership decisions at work:

▸ Asking for opportunities

▸ Seeking opportunities

▸ Creating opportunities

Asking for Opportunities

Once we gain awareness in how we define leadership and how the organizations and people we work for define and find value in leaders and their practice, the most natural thing we can do for ourselves to practice is to ask for the opportunity to do so. We can ask for opportunities to practice from our manager. We can ask for opportunities to practice with our peers. We can ask for opportunities with our teams.

We can ask to lead projects. We can vocalize this desire to those who can make the decisions to give us the opportunities to practice our leadership. In hoping that you work for an organization that supports you, you can begin to grow each day in having the opportunity to practice. The beauty of asking for these opportunities is the initiative that we show when asking to take on more. That looks good. That changes perceptions. People like those of us who ask for opportunities. That, within itself, can position us as leaders in the workplace. It can be scary to ask for the opportunity. It presents a level of taking action in wanting to make a change and positioning ourselves.

Asking may also present a level of vulnerability if we work with or for people who may not support our leadership decisions. What if our manager says no? What if our peer doesn't want to collaborate? What if my team isn't supportive? What if it doesn't work out? What if I look foolish? Those are all minor risks and risks we should take to practice. A piece of the best advice I've heard in doing career development training was, "Don't let your manager be a roadblock to your career."

In building on that quote, we can't let people stop us from deciding to practice our leadership. We need to feel supported enough and sure enough to ask for opportunities to practice and not depend on the approval of others. We need to work with and for people who believe in us enough to say yes when we ask for or present opportunity. Let's consider a few scenarios.

In the first, let's say that you are a manager of a small team of five people. One day, one of your average team members asks to be on more projects and to work with you more directly to learn more about your job role. You say yes feeling surprised and excited that this person is taking initiative and showing gumption to be more involved and to contribute more.

You introduce them to some of your colleagues across the organization and begin to hear excellent feedback about what they are contributing to these new projects. Overall, in giving this person more responsibility because they asked, you are excited to see this person flourish. Even in your meetings with them, you notice a change in their attitude and behavior. Your perception of this person begins to change over time, and you start to rely on them more.

The other four team members don't ask to do more, so come promotion time, one name stands out in your mind, and it's the name of the person who asked to do more. They took a chance to ask. They proved themselves through their practice. They were formally promoted.

Now that you've considered the manager's point of view, imagine that you are the employee. You've grown bored in your role and want to advance. In talking to people across the organization, you learn that your manager and the organization as a whole values initiative and people who ask for what they want. Being somewhat scared to talk to your manager about taking on more work, but also knowing that you can't sit idly watching your career stall, you make the decision one day to ask to do more. Your manager seems surprised, but happily suggests and provides new opportunities.

Your team members notice and two of them admit they admire the "new you" while the other two neither support nor acknowledge the steps you are taking. You feel secure enough in your decision, though, knowing that you want the perception of yourself to change. You want to do more and want to be perceived as more than average to enhance your career.

In asking, you begin to meet people once you get involved in new projects. Your confidence grows, and you find people seeking you out for your advice. You gain exposure to top leaders within the organization and one day are thrilled when your manager gives you a promotion. The simple decision to ask for an opportunity to do more worked in your favor.

In asking and finding new ways to do more, you were able to practice leading through various avenues in considering collaborating, managing time, and enhancing your understanding of the organization and its goals. Practice is key to behavior change. It is why we need to ask for opportunities to practice each day. We need to feel that we can ask.

If you are in a formal leadership role now, ensure that your team members feel safe in approaching you to find more ways to practice their leadership at work. Some of the saddest stories I hear are when people leave organizations because their manager didn't support them with their growth as a leader. They decided to go somewhere else that would.

No company or manager should consider that an ideal situation. The best leaders encourage their employees to develop their leadership ability while also developing themselves. We also need to decide for ourselves to ask for opportunities and to practice.

Seeking Opportunities

Along with asking for the opportunity, we can also seek out leadership opportunities to help us practice. This is different from asking. When asking, we commit the ask and, most likely, ask for an opportunity from our managers, team members, or peers. It can add a formality in the exposure.

When we seek opportunity, we become opportunity detectives. We invite the opportunity to practice to find us in asking those around us to collaborate or unite efforts. We may not know what we want to ask for formally from our manager. We may not feel comfortable doing that. We may not want to quite commit in full by asking either.

In seeking opportunity, we can leave our options open to see what comes to us at the right time from others we work with and what they are pursuing. In getting comfortable with knowing that, we need to talk to people to gain awareness, to obtain evaluation and feedback, and to hear perspective.

We also need to get comfortable with talking to people to learn what they are doing and how piggybacking on their projects can give us the opportunity we need to practice leading. Seeking people out whom we work with and asking questions can help us find these opportunities to practice. Ask questions like these:

▸ What do you do all day?

▸ What are you working on today that's of high value and/or priority?

▸ What's keeping you up at night?

▶ What's your biggest current challenge?

▶ What projects could we potentially partner on?

Seeking enables us to connect with others. Seeking also invites the opportunity to work with new people. Asking lets people know they can turn to us if something comes up that we can collaborate with them on. Plus, it also shows that we care. Sure, we may be wanting to seek opportunities for our leadership growth, but another benefit of that is how it connects us with others we may not have connected with previously.

It can be scary to seek feedback and then ask people these sorts of questions depending on how close we are with them. It helps in positioning ourselves, changing perceptions, and creating an opportunity for when the time is right. It also opens us up for more opportunity.

Consider this example. Fred is a director of accounting and has been in this role for ten years. He feels himself getting bored and notices his motivation is dwindling. Feeling a bit unsure of what to do and hesitant to speak to his manager, Donna, about his feelings, he decides to talk to his colleagues within finance to learn more about what they are working on. He hopes that finding something new to work on with someone else on the team will help him reengage at work.

Fred also hopes it will help him move up the formal leadership ladder from director to the senior director as he's looking to refine his leadership skills after receiving feedback from his manager that he is lacking in organizing and managing global teams. In talking to his peers on what they are working on, Fred discovers that the vice president of finance, Mohammad, is working on some new global initiatives to enhance teamwork across the finance team.

Fred is intrigued and asks Mohammad if the two can collaborate as he has some ideas on where improvements can be made. Mohammad agrees as he's happy to help Fred and appreciates the extra help with his effort. In seeking people out, Fred can practice organizing and managing teams across the globe with the help of Mohammad. In doing this, he builds a relationship with Henry who helps him fine-tune his abilities in these areas.

Fred is then able to report back to Donna about his work. She is impressed that Fred took the steps he needed to practice this skill and is also pleased when Henry also provides her with feedback on Fred's success. The following year, she grants Fred the promotion he so severely wants due to his effort and practice. Without seeking this out and talking to his peers, Fred may have never learned about the opportunity with Mohammad that aided in his leadership practice.

Creating Opportunities

Nell is midtwenties and ambitious. She works in research and development for a software company. She learns about

Toastmasters from a friend at another organization and hears about the value that this program offers people in enhancing their communication and leadership skills.

After a company function one afternoon, she decides to ask the CEO if he will support Toastmasters coming to their organization. He wants to know more and asks Nell to schedule a meeting to discuss further. After hearing Nell's case, he also sees the value and agrees to support Nell and her mission of bringing Toastmasters to the company. In organizing, along with managing her full-time job responsibilities, she

▶ Invited people to join her cause and motivated them to do so,

▶ Secured budget, rooms, and resources to ensure its success, and

▶ Marketed the program and its benefits to the organization to gain members.

So what did Nell do? Ultimately, she created an opportunity to lead. She created it for herself. Nell decided to act and followed through. In starting a Toastmasters program at her workplace, she was able to practice her leadership both in bringing the program into the organization and further practice within the scope of the program.

Nell created an opportunity for herself to lead at work. She found something she believed in and acted. She positioned herself as a leader to those across the organization and to the CEO. Depending on where you work, this may be easier said than done in being able to create your opportunities. You could push yourself to create opportunity and to ask to do so. That, within itself, is practicing leadership. Give thought to the following:

▸ How can you create opportunities at work to practice your leadership?

▸ Where is there a gap within the organization that you could fill in leading a project, program, or initiative?

▸ What else can you do within your organization to create opportunities for yourself and those whom you work with?

Creating opportunity can take various paths. The point is to create something where you can practice and add value. In doing that, we position ourselves in the minds and perceptions of others of being leaders. Could you do something similar to what Nell did in bringing in a program?

When we make the decisions to act, that's when we practice. That's when we lead. When we create our opportunity to lead, we challenge the perceptions of those around us. We drive our development. We position our brand and define our lifestyle. We decide to lead. In summarizing what we've discussed, we can practice being leaders and in making the decisions by

▶ Asking for opportunities directly from those above us or around us,

▶ Seeking out opportunities from those we work with across the organizations in talking to our peers to see where and how we can align ourselves with them and their initiatives, and

▶ Creating our opportunities where we see need to position ourselves and to aid our peers and our organization.

Now that we've talked about work let's look at other ways we can practice our Leadership Lifestyle outside of the office.

Outside of the Job

If we are trying to live a Leadership Lifestyle, we need to practice our leadership outside of the confines of work. There are many ways to practice and lots of ways we can make decisions too. Even if you don't work a regular job, you can still benefit from the A/P/E Model and make decisions about your leadership.

Whether you are a student, a stay-at-home parent, or a nontraditional worker, anyone can be a leader and find ways to practice. Let's say you have an idea for an app and don't know where to start. Do you want to create something?

You think you can do a better job than someone else? Here's your chance.

Gain awareness. Practice writing a business plan. Solicit and find team members to buy into your vision. What makes it special? Why should they be involved? Leaders need to tell these stories every day, and here's an opportunity to practice. I say app as an example, but the same can apply to any other venture. We get stuck in our lives and moments. As we know, life changes. We need to find ways to build ourselves. We need to find ways to practice. One day we could have that job or be in school, and the next day everything could change. A pandemic could arrive.

Let's say that you're a stay-at-home parent and your partner loses their job. You now need to find a job to support the household but haven't worked in years. That could hurt you when looking. Luckily, even though you weren't working a formal career, you still found ways to lead. When updating your resume, you fill it with leading community projects, school functions, and volunteering. In finding ways to make decisions about our leadership and considering our ventures, we can find ways to practice outside of our job and grow our development in our own ways.

We can volunteer. We can lead a special interest group. We can work another job for fun. We can give back. We can lead by example in all of these situations. Leadership is not only for those in the corporate world. It's for everyone no matter where they are in life. It's just up to us to find that opportunity and use it to our benefit to grow. Let's look at each one of these opportunities more in-depth in the ways that we can use each to practice our leadership. In each of the examples of ways we can practice in the coming pages, we can

▸ Ask for opportunities,

▸ Seek opportunities, and

▸ Create opportunities.

Regardless of what you decide to do, what matters is that you are making the decision to practice and then deciding to follow through in doing so outside of the confines of work for yourself and your development.

Volunteer

One way that we can practice leadership outside of work is through volunteering. Whether that is at the local hospital, for the local government, or with an association, we can find ways to give back while practicing our leadership behaviors. The hard part of incorporating this is managing the time. If we're working full-time or raising kids at home full-time, plus managing friends and family, it can be a challenge to incorporate volunteering into our lifestyle. It can be an option that helps to build our Leadership Brand further while giving us the opportunity to practice. It also helps to change perceptions.

In managing perceptions, volunteering shows others that we have a cause that we care enough about to dedicate our time. Volunteering can also help us meet new people. New people with diverse backgrounds can help us gain perspective. That within itself can help us in making decisions and gaining awareness to aid more in our development. It can also give us the chance to do things that we like doing. If we like helping animals, for example, and that makes us feel good about ourselves, we should practice leading in scenarios that unite both. Plenty of websites detail volunteering opportunities. Local organizations and associations in your community may also provide opportunities.

Similar to asking an organization formally to volunteer, we can also seek opportunities in asking those around us about their causes and missions. You could even create your mission or group if you see a need not being met in the community. That, too, can help us practice our leadership ability in creating a vision and then logistically planning the steps to launch.

Volunteering provides us with an opportunity to practice. It gives us chances to practice what we may fear practicing at work for whatever our reason may be. Greta Thunberg comes to mind as an example in the work she's done around climate change with her #FridaysForFuture, which is a movement that began in August 2018 after she and other young activists sat in front of the Swedish parliament every school day for three weeks to protest against the lack of action on the climate crisis. She posted what she was doing on Twitter and it soon went viral. This was her decision to lead through volunteering.

Lead a Special Interest Group

Building on the idea of volunteering, you could also join or create a special interest group. The beauty in leading a special interest group is that you can develop something based on your interests while creating a practice opportunity. It can fall into the volunteering bucket, but may also be created for the sake of uniting people for a common interest or goal.

Let's say you have a specific interest; how about knitting? Knitting with a group wouldn't be a volunteering endeavor, and you may not get paid to knit, which I will cover in the next part. It is a way for you to unite people and to practice your leadership ability. Think about this in creating a vision of the group and plan, market, and organize logistics.

In doing that, you can also unite people while recruiting people to your Feedback Board and Success Team. We will discuss both later on. You can gather people in a way that blends, challenges, and convenes for a common goal or interest. This could also be a resume builder in gathering people together for a common cause or interest. It's a way to gather more people into your circle to network and talk.

In talking to people, we can expand our growth and knowledge about ourselves and thus increase our awareness. Specifically, in uniting people, we can learn. In learning, we grow. As an example of this, I worked with a man, Rupert, who in 2008 was laid off from a major US financial firm along with 500 other people. Feeling frustrated and unsure of what to do next while also battling less-than-ideal job market conditions, he asked a few of his peers who were also laid off to meet for coffee at a local diner.

That one coffee meeting turned into a weekly gathering where those in similar circumstances to Rupert spent time helping one another with resumes, introducing each other to contacts to help with networking, and overall supporting each other as needed in finding new jobs. A few weeks into the meetings and due to a great deal of word of mouth, the small weekly group meeting outgrew the coffee shop and expanded into the basement of the local library.

In growing, the focus of the weekly meetings changed and now guest speakers were lecturing, and more and more networking was happening. Months later, the library basement became too small, and the group moved to a local hotel that provided a conference room for the hundreds now in attendance at no cost. Local media covered what Rupert and his group were doing to help people with their career search.

A year or so after the group started, Rupert found a job and went back to work. Rupert had led a great initiative that helped people find jobs, network, and develop. It also helped him create his leadership opportunity for himself to practice and to lead. He saw a need and acted.

A "Fun" Job

Earlier, I talked about traditional ways to practice in explicitly looking at the working world. We can also practice through what I'm calling a fun job. A fun job is a job outside of the nine-to-five. Fun jobs could include

- Kayak guide

- Adjunct lecturing

- Bike tour guide

These jobs differ from volunteering as you'd most likely get some financial gain. Each can be labeled as fun because they are outside of the typical workplace and can align with a particular hobby or interest that you may have. In having one of these opportunities and working with the timing to manage, we can find other ways to practice with diverse groups of people while doing something we like, or love. For these, we can ask for, seek out, or create an opportunity.

Let's use the kayak guide example. Here, you get to teach people how to paddle a kayak, manage their safety, motivate them when they feel frustrated, and lead by example in the way that you paddle. Teaching can be another way to give back while learning and practicing yourself. We could approach this in teaching at the local community education program, local college or university, or online.

What matters in all of these opportunities is that you have an outlet outside of the daily grind to try something new while also challenging yourself in new ways to build your awareness while practicing. That outlet, within itself, can help in your overall growth. These opportunities, in thinking more about the technical and work environment, can aid in building your resume by filling it with other ways to demonstrate your leadership potential and lifestyle through your decisions and dedication.

I found this approach to be beneficial myself because I am an adjunct lecturer. In that medium, I could practice different areas of leadership that I wanted to experiment with in a new setting outside of work to gain confidence before applying or testing during my full-time role. My students didn't know me, so I could be whatever persona I wanted to be in that setting in defining myself and my value as a leader in teaching.

If in one class I wanted to practice being more direct with my delivery, I could and commit to practicing throughout the duration of the semester. If I wanted to practice empathy and my ability to connect with people, I could find ways to practice that. I could then apply those skills to my full-time role once building my confidence.

I decided to practice taking action. It was also fun for me. I like teaching and working with students. I found joy in public speaking and in educating students on whatever topic I was instructing at the time. It gave me something to look forward to where I felt like I was making a difference outside of the regular paycheck job while also earning a little extra money within the gig economy.

What matters, though, is that I found this opportunity and made the time for it, which helped me in developing myself in more ways than I could have imagined. This is where I challenge you to think about where you can find a fun job, or any opportunity to practice. In doing that, you'll also gain more awareness about yourself through practice and exploration.

With regard to evaluation, I gained this insight through the feedback of my students at the end of the semester, but also made a point to ask for feedback throughout to further develop and challenge myself as an instructor. The same could apply to the kayak guide job. Hearing feedback, learning from new people, having fun while building new leadership skill sets—all can work to your benefit.

We don't need to stick to our work jobs or whatever that may look like to you to practice our leadership through our decisions. We can seek other opportunities that also support our Leadership Lifestyle and what we are trying to accomplish for ourselves. The decision is ours to do this. This decision is ours to prioritize these tasks with our other leadership decisions on a day-to-day basis. Once deciding to practice, finding ways to do so, and then practicing, we may even surprise ourselves with what we develop out of it.

9

Evaluation

I was holding a leadership training and found that one of my students was getting irritated with my optimistic messages of the importance of feedback as a way to evaluate one's efforts. I found myself getting more and more distracted by his fidgeting and agitated looks.

"What's on your mind?" I finally asked him.

"I feel I should be promoted to VP," Tim, director of sales, told the class. He wasn't getting promoted, and he couldn't understand why, year after year. He desperately wanted that formal recognition of his leadership capabilities through that promotion. After sharing his frustrations and detailing how every year his sales exceeded the sales of his peers, the class and I sat there stunned.

A few days later, I ran into Tim's manager. My curiosity got the best of me. I had to ask, "Why did Tim never get promoted?"

The manager answered simply, "All he cares about are his numbers. He doesn't care about the team or his peers at that level, and he doesn't receive feedback well or ask for it. I try to tell him that, but he just won't listen."

So that was it. It came down to Tim's lacking awareness. He merely needed the awareness and the feedback to help himself, which he wasn't receiving or realizing. It didn't matter about his sales numbers. What mattered were the relationships that he had with others. Tim had no interest in forming or changing the relationships with those around him, which is what the company valued in leaders. He dismissed feedback that could have been helpful to him.

Which brings us to the final piece of the A/P/E Model: evaluation.

Evaluation is the glue that sticks the other pieces of the cycle together in showing how your hard work is paying off and your initiative is being perceived. Alternatively, it can be the kick in the butt you need to continue to expand your awareness, to practice differently, and to change your behavior. Or it can be blah, blah, blah depending on how you understand it or not, like who it's coming from.

Evaluation can be scary. It's scary to hear that your hard work isn't paying off. Feedback can be frightening. Performance ratings can be dreadful. It can be exciting and empowering when people around you see a difference in you and the way you lead and the evaluation you hear is positive. Your decisions and work are paying off.

I will discuss evaluation and the way that we can use it and feedback as a tool to gauge our practice. This chapter will further align with the awareness section as the two work hand in hand. In evaluating our efforts and making a decision to seek feedback to gauge our progress, we will address

▶ Defining feedback and understanding traditional mediums,

▶ Creating and using a Success Team and Feedback Board to gain feedback and evaluation in our Leadership Lifestyle, and

▶ Looking internally to assess our efforts through self-evaluation.

Let's first look at feedback in the traditional sense and gain an understanding of what feedback, or evaluation, is.

Defining and Understanding Feedback

Feedback, as tied to evaluation, can be difficult for people to pursue in their self-evaluation of their practice through their leadership decisions in line with the A/P/E Model. When we think of feedback, we believe that we are doing something wrong. We need to remember that feedback can also be positive. It can be a celebration of our successes and our achievements. We've tied feedback too much to this idea of grading and not of a learning tool. We need to reframe feedback.

Some, justly, link feedback with performance management. Yes, during performance management discussions, you receive formal feedback about your work performance over the duration of a year from your manager. Yes, some companies still do this while others are moving away from this model and encouraging employees to give feedback to one another more frequently to aid in culture change while also enhancing productivity and engagement.

Feedback-rich environments, which we can look at as being workplace cultures where feedback is given and received on a regular basis, can have significant benefits to both the organization and to those who are employed by it. In tying this to our Leadership Brand mission and lifestyle, feedback and evaluation can give us insight on whether our decisions are driving our behavior change that can position us as leaders, or not.

I often train on giving and receiving feedback best practices. I do this to challenge people and the way that we think about feedback. Most of this training is linked to performance management, but much ties back to how the best get better and how those who are successful in formal leadership roles were able to use feedback to their advantage. The best get better in knowing how to get feedback and use it for their development and growth.

In talking about feedback, I challenge those who take my courses to go out and ask their peers or organizational leaders for their feedback, to hear the perceptions that people have of them. In asking people to do this, what do you think their reaction is? They say no. They can't do this. They are too scared. They are too afraid of what people will tell them and how they will react in hearing those perceptions.

Some people, and top organizational leaders, have done this process throughout their careers and attribute their success to this practice. They've learned how to adapt and flex based on the feedback they've received to help them grow as a leader. Because of that, they may often give feedback to others by hoping to help them grow and succeed. In thinking about how you can become a better receiver of feedback to improve your leadership and your leadership decisions about your practice, let's examine a few points to keep in mind that can help us reframe feedback so we can better use it to evaluate our leadership decisions and their impact:

- ▶ Feedback is only someone's opinion and an opinion based on a perception and, sometimes, misperceptions.

- ▶ It's an opinion about your behavior—at least it should be. Feedback shouldn't be about someone's attitude or our own bias about who they are as a person.

▶ Feedback should be behavior based. Sometimes, we may need to hear feedback that is about our attitude or what we show others about who we are. Sometimes we need to make changes to our personality or the way that we treat people to be more effective.

In thinking about that, you, as the receiver, can begin to frame feedback in a way that's more useful. It's an opinion that we could benefit from hearing for our own growth. What if someone went on Yelp and wrote a terrible review of your favorite restaurant and criticized each and every menu aspect that you love about it—the service, the staff, and, most importantly, the food?

Would that make you stop going? What if you ate at a place that was terrible? Service was bad. Servers were rude and the food! Gosh, the food was terrible. When you check Yelp, that same person raved and raved about this restaurant, and it was their favorite. Would that change your perception of the place?

Earlier on, I talked about how perception is reality. Your reality can't be debated and neither can someone else's. We experience restaurants like we experience others, based on our background, our perceptions, and thereby our reality. It is how we give feedback based on our perceptions, our opinions, and our realities. Are you going to let one bad Yelp review change the way that you view and enjoy a particular restaurant? Probably not. The same goes for feedback.

However, if person after person starts telling you the same thing about the same restaurant, that's another story. That's a trend, and that trend becomes data. If you are receiving the same piece of feedback time and time again, that can signal an area for improvement. We can't let one piece of feedback hinder our efforts. We can hear it, make a decision about its usefulness, and then decide how worthy it is in our evaluation of our efforts.

For any growth, we need to listen to what's said. What's the real message? We know that opinions from one person can mean a lot, depending on the person, or mean very little, depending on the person. If person after person is giving us the same kind of feedback, we need to listen. We especially need to hear the feedback if we want to improve as leaders.

Feedback not only helps us see where we can improve and what we've improved on, but it also helps us become better at assisting other people to develop as we've developed a healthy attitude and practice. It helps to toughen our skin as leaders to open ourselves to others. In addition, feedback not only toughens that skin but helps us forge new relationships with people while adding to their success and our own.

As you develop your Success Team, you'll begin to learn which people you can get accurate and honest feedback from in a way that further supports your development. We all have an ego—some more than others. It's important to know that in any feedback exercise. We need to listen. It shows respect. Knowing when to sit back and let others share their thoughts and expertise can be a test of our leadership.

No one ever said a great leader or even an influential one is a person who never listens. Performance management, which I will address in the next section, is one way we can hear feedback about ourselves, and typically within the traditional workplace setting. Within the work world, we can utilize 360-degree feedback, or what some people call multi-rater feedback, to hear how our colleagues are experiencing our decisions and behavior.

You may be wondering why this matters. Even though leadership is up to us to make the decisions in our lives, we can use this traditional resource to gain awareness about what we need to do to aid in our decision-making and practice. In knowing that, how can you begin to rethink the way you think about feedback? Let's examine this first in thinking about the traditional method within the work setting—performance management.

Creating and Using a Success Team and Feedback Board

You are deciding to take initiative through your decisions to enhance your leadership by reading this book. You want to be a leader or a better leader whether at work, at home/ life, or for an extracurricular activity. You feel the need to lead in your life and want to live a lifestyle that reflects this decision. Maybe you are reading this book because you want to find ways to improve yourself overall. Whatever the case may be, the one who cares about you becoming a better leader is you. You are the one who needs to make the decisions to change your behavior and to make decisions about your development. But you can't do it alone.

Leaders need people. Not just people to lead, but people to help them lead. Most people don't care about your development. You may come across the occasional peer, mentor, or manager who truly cares about you and your progress. Finding people who truly care about you and your development are rare. If you do come across someone who cares about you and your leadership development, hold on to them tightly with both hands. Figuratively speaking.

Why? As the saying goes, "People want to see you do well, but never better than them." Having people around you who have your best interest in mind and like you (remember TOLL) helps your development and your success. As a leader, it's crucial for you to find people that you can trust to support you and your leadership decisions.

You need to make people want to give a crap about you. People who impress those around them and show respect and humility while working hard often engender strong support from those around them. This can lead to more frequent and more useful feedback. A mutual trust develops between people that then supports a mutual reliance. In knowing that leadership is a lifestyle, finding and nurturing relationships with those in your life, both at work and at home, who can help you evaluate your efforts is essential to your growth. Your perspective about yourself and your development will only take you so far. It is why you need others to help you.

In this section, I present to you two groups of people you need to create as a way to evaluate your decisions. You need to form these groups to help you with your lifestyle and your awareness and self-evaluation, which will enable you to make better leadership decisions. The groups are

▶ A Success Team and

▶ A Feedback Board.

Your Success Team should be composed of a few people whom you consider mentors and people who care about you a lot. I deem a few as three. These people need to give a crap about you. This team could be made up of family members, friends, work leaders, people whom you admire, or those you consider mentors.

To make your Success Team care about you, you do so by building a relationship with them, asking them about their own life and struggles and finding time to connect. These people should have one goal, and that goal is seeing you be successful as a leader. I note that mentors should be a part of this team. When people think about mentors, they often think they need just one. One can only help you to an extent.

Mentorship along with Success Teams and Feedback Boards shouldn't be monogamous. If you have a "team" of mentors, it helps to broaden your network and perspective. It is why we need a team behind us. Your Success Team, although small, should be diverse. Diversity helps us to make better decisions about our leadership.

Diversity helps us hear perspectives and feedback we may have never considered before. Diversity helps us enhance our practice and deepen our awareness when we hear evaluation from these people. It means that if you are a twenty-eight-year-old White male working in finance, your Success Team should not be made up of other twenty-eight-year-old White males who also work in finance.

That is not diversity and not going to help you. People who are younger, older, different industries, backgrounds, genders, ethnicities along with a mix of professional and personal contacts are going to give that team more strength than one mentor alone can provide. These are people you could talk with quarterly or monthly to gain their feedback. Whatever the cadence is, it should be consistent. You need to integrate talking to these people as part of your Leadership Lifestyle. Having diverse people who care about your success and who see you in action would be best. But that's a tough mix to find and requires you to be very active in recruiting up-to-date mentors.

Second, you need to have a Feedback Board. I suggest that you have three to five people who can support you in this fashion. Similar to that of a board of advisors, a Feedback Board provides you with just that—feedback. The group can be composed of people from work, academia, associations, family, or friends. The list of potentials goes on and on. They don't need to give as much of a crap about you as your Success Team, but you need to be able to ask them for feedback and perspective in thinking about your growth and practice.

The goal of the Feedback Board is to educate you on how they perceive your behavior and should have exposure to you when you are leading. They need to give you feedback in an honest way. I'll talk about that more in the next section. These people aren't as deep as your Success Team but should care about you and your development enough to take the time to give you the evaluations you need to aid in your growth.

You may want to include people you don't like, or people you know don't like you. I say this as these people may be the ones who can give you the feedback that spurs you to the point of making true behavior change. People who don't like you can be the ones who give you the most accurate perceptions compared to those you have deeper relationships with who may shy away from being completely honest for fear of damaging the relationship.

Your Feedback Board and Success Team should have members mixed from both your personal and professional worlds as a way to give you feedback that can help you grow as a person and as a leader. I suggest family and friends to an extent. You may not want your mother and father, but you could have family members who could provide more balanced and caring feedback than anyone else. I also suggest friends depending on how and where they've seen you lead and what their perception and experiences have been with that. I have friends who have a keen business sense. They also know and care about me. I want them on my team because of both of these aspects.

You want these people involved in your practice, but you should always be thinking about whether or not you need to swap out members of each group to keep perspectives new, to help in challenging yourself and building your network. You may also swap out if you suddenly find that someone isn't available for professional or personal reasons. If you notice that a member is having difficulties at work or at home that could hinder your growth, you may not actually "fire" these people from your board, but you can find ways to sunset them out while finding new people to help you.

There's a saying that I've heard that resonates with these points. It goes, "Birds of a feather flock together." Another popular one is, "You are judged by the company you keep." This supports a level of awareness in that, at work or home, if you associate yourself with the wrong people, it could hurt your growth, your reputation, and the way that others perceive you.

Whatever the case may be, it's something to be aware of when gaining feedback and including people on these teams. Use your best judgment when making changes or including new people. When recruiting or deciding to make a change, remember the importance of informational interviewing to gain perspective for yourself in interviewing and learning from others.

The Importance of Honesty

The stereotype about millennials is that they've been given a trophy for everything in their life. They've grown up with positive reinforcement and have participation awards for everything they've ever attempted. Other generations look at this trend and laugh.

Why do others laugh? Because sometimes you need tough love. Brutal honesty. A good kick in the butt. You want people on both your Success Team and Feedback Board to be honest with you. At times, you may need a kick in the butt from these people to make a change in your practice and to become a leader.

Have you ever had someone give you brutally honest feedback? How was it delivered? How did it make you feel? What did you learn? Why does this matter? It matters because sometimes we need to be told that we suck at something. That we suck more than anyone else at that particular task or skill. That our efforts aren't working, that something needs to change if we want to be an effective leader.

We may need to hear that feedback from either people we like, or not, on either team to make a behavior change and evaluate our efforts to help with our overall leadership growth and to make better decisions. Sometimes having someone tell us that we are failing can be what we need to succeed. There's also a balance here. Consider the situation like this:

▶ We need to ask for feedback in order to get it.

▶ Sometimes people aren't good at giving feedback, which can become a stressor for the feedback giver in not being clear or honest in their message.

▶ It can be difficult to translate feedback into an actionable message on what we need to do to change our behavior to be more effective.

You can say no to feedback from people you don't admire or respect. Don't let that bad energy drain you. You may want to take it back to your teams to see if they agree that it's something you could work on in the future. I have heard feedback about myself that I don't agree with from people on my teams and from others whom I've worked or interacted with personally.

Sometimes that feedback can drain you more than you want to admit. The decision that you need to make is how you want to handle it. You can dwell on the feedback and let it fester to the point that you feel like you are going insane. Or you can decide to wipe it from your mind. One person said one thing about you one time. That does not define you as a person or as a leader. If it does fester inside and the feedback lingers and lingers, stop and think about that. Is it telling you something about yourself that you may not want to admit? The more data, or information, the better. The more honest feedback we hear, whether we agree, or not, can be the tool we need to make decisions to be better leaders.

Self-Evaluating Our Leadership Decisions

Whom do you trust the most in the world? When I answer that question, I say myself. Yes, I trust my family. I trust my friends. I trust those on my Feedback and Success teams. I trust my manager. But I trust myself the most.

When it comes to our leadership development, we can only trust people to an extent when it comes to our evaluation regardless of how much we think they care. It's also the reality and the awareness that situations change. People change. Relationships change. We change especially if we are growing.

It is why we may need to swap people out of our teams. It is also why we must learn to find ways to self-evaluate our leadership decisions in how we feel. Utilizing traditional work-based methods helps, like 360-degree feedback or performance management, in gaining evaluation and awareness. Turning to those on our Success Team and Feedback Board can give us further perspective.

When we think about leadership and the related decisions to our Leadership Lifestyle, we need to learn to self-evaluate and trust ourselves in doing that. How do we feel? Do we think that things are changing? Do we feel like a leader? Having a level of self-awareness with this can help us further work with and understand the way that others may perceive us. It can help us improve ourselves.

You bought this book because you are deciding to make a step to improve yourself for yourself. Learning how to trust ourselves and practice evaluating our efforts can take work. It can be a difficult practice as it can be challenging to look at ourselves objectively. We're all perfect, right? There are various ways that we can do this. Let's look further while keeping in mind we are all responsible and accountable for our own behavior and our decisions.

How You Feel: The Good Feelings

Being able to lead and influence people is exhilarating. In thinking back about why people want to be leaders, this sense or feeling of success can be a primary driver. The last way that we can self-evaluate is taking time to think about how we feel in the overall sense. Some people are in touch with their feelings and well-being, yet some find themselves struggling with being able to do this. It is why meditation and journaling can help us connect with ourselves.

Take time to stop and ask yourself, "How do I feel about my leadership decisions today?" This self-assessment can be that brief moment of check-in that you need to align your decisions for the day with your lifestyle. When we begin this practice of taking the time to stop and ask ourselves this, we can look internally and determine whether the work is paying off or not simply by understanding how we feel. Do we notice a difference? Are we more content? Do we see changes in ourselves? Why does this matter? It matters because this is about you. You are reading this book for you. You want to change for you. If something's not working for you, you need to see it, understand it, and then improve it. You need to evaluate how you feel and to gauge if your practice is making a difference or not.

Taking the time to stop and self-evaluate is a simple decision we can make each day. If you put all this work into something and it's not working for you, stop. If your conditions are making life and leadership too hard, change them. Depending on your circumstances, this could be difficult. If you can find a way, find a way. Decide to do so for yourself. It does not mean that if something gets hard with your leadership decisions you stop.

I once heard a CEO say, in thinking about how to grow in business, "You need to get comfortable with being uncomfortable." Why? It helps you develop. We don't grow and improve by doing the same thing over and over again and expecting a different outcome.

We need to be in tune with ourselves to notice changes. We need to be in tune with ourselves to celebrate ourselves and our efforts. We need to feel good about what we do. Once we think that, we'll continue to grow and work hard. Once we're sick of it, we're sick of it and need to find something else to practice to help. It is about you. You need to feel good about the decisions that you make and the impact that your decisions have in your life. Once you stop feeling good or stop seeing your efforts pay off in a way that makes you feel good, you need to make a change. That's awareness. That's leadership. That's self-evaluation. That's a decision.

If things are going well and you feel good, and the feedback is good, and you see changes for the positive, then that's what matters for you and your path. From that, you can feel good about the decisions that you've made and the difference that those decisions have made to you. We can take more holistic approaches to judging our own internal feelings as leaders through meditation, yoga, or journaling. What's important is that we, as leaders, are taking time to consider how we feel about our Leadership Lifestyle and our decisions.

How You Feel: The Bad Feelings

What comes to mind when you think about the word *failure*? A time you failed? The exact moment? Maybe the feelings that you had during that moment? Were they shame? Anger? Frustration? Maybe you felt like you've never failed. Is that true? It's not. We've all failed at some point. Failure can be the keys we need to succeed.

At some points during our lives and careers, we've all failed at something regardless of who we are. Let's face it. Nothing has ever gone perfectly, for anyone. Failure can be one of the greatest learning tools available. It can be the most significant way we self-evaluate based on the way we feel. Sure, take a class. Read a book. Failure shows that you tried at something. Not just read about it.

In failing, you practiced. You took the chance. You failed. You learned. You will try again. You've gained awareness on how you will do it differently next time. The word itself lends itself to admit that the risk we took may not have turned out in the way that we wanted it to, but at least we tried.

Leadership is messy. It's about working with people. It's about working on yourself. If we don't fail in thinking about our leadership and decisions, we are doing something wrong. It's difficult to admit to failure. It can be empowering to recognize when you fail instead of trying to cover it up.

What would you rather have someone do when working with you? I think that most would rather have someone admit to failure than lie about it and attempt to cover it up. That lends itself to the perception of being an honest leader and a trusted brand.

When it comes to failing at leadership, though, we need to define what failure looks like and if we can fail at leadership. Can we fail at leadership? That depends. If we define leadership in the way that we view leaders and in knowing that perception is reality, can we ever accurately say that someone failed at leadership? Is it an opportunity in growth in thinking about another level of awareness and evaluation to thereby practice?

Admitting to failure, ironically enough, can be one of those trick questions asked in interviews masked in this exchange:

Interviewer: "Tell me about a time you failed."

Interviewee (trying to look good): "I've never failed at anything."

Interviewer: "Really? You've never failed at anything? Surely there must be something. Heck, I can name a few moments in my life when I failed. Nothing comes to mind?"

You may have lived that exchange as either one or the other person in thinking about the nature of that conversation. It's an interesting one. It teaches us about our decision-making skills and the ability to make said decisions. We can learn that maybe sometimes we don't think that we know all that we do. We will learn a lot about the relationships around us and how people view us and our leadership ability. Plus, for our brand, it shows that we are honest.

Whether you practice at work or outside of work, it's not always going to work out. From that, you can learn. You will gain new awareness from this. You could find a new way to practice and then evaluate, which I will address in the next part of this book. In acknowledging failure and the feelings that come with it, that can be the most significant and most influential way that we self-evaluate. It can be challenging to do. It can be the push we need to self-evaluate to enhance our practice.

Bad feelings with leadership can also take the face of being let down by someone we trusted, or letting those around us down. Those bad feelings can be guides to our decisions moving forward in how we define value for ourselves and in others and how we use this knowledge to reframe our decisions.

Summarizing the A/P/E Model

Now that we understand the A/P/E Model in its entirety, we can see how each element of the cycle provides a framework in which we can make decisions to lead and to take the initiative to do so. We can also see how the three elements work with one another. In aligning TOLL to enhance our leadership decisions and lifestyle further, we can make decisions to use

▶ Timing to become more effective as leaders,

▶ Opportunity to open ourselves to new experiences,

▶ Looks in how we define how we look and feel as leaders, and

▶ Likes in how we feel about ourselves and the support around us.

This is alignment between the two models—A/P/E and TOLL—at a high level. However, it provides a summary of the ways that the two models work together. In giving both models consideration, we can apply either to our own lives to help us make our own decisions. As we move into the next part, we will look into the attributes, skills, and behaviors that we can unite with the models to enhance our decisions and lifestyle.

PART III:

Evaluating Leadership Attributes, Skills, and Behaviors to Make Leadership Decisions

"Become the kind of leader that people would follow voluntarily, even if you had no title or position. Conduct a personal assessment and ask yourself, 'Would I follow me?'"

Brian Tracy

10

Evaluating Leadership Attributes, Skills, and Behaviors

In understanding the A/P/E Model along with TOLL, we can use both to frame our decisions about our leadership. Let's examine the attributes, skills, and behaviors that we evaluate leaders by and can utilize for ourselves in further developing our leadership ability through our decisions. In gaining awareness, we can determine what makes sense for us to practice in our own lives as leaders.

When we began, I asked you to define leadership and what makes a leader, a leader along with detailing how you find value in those who lead. The list of attributes, skills, and behaviors that make leaders can number in the thousands. Some books and consultants create assessments, lists, and content to distill to just a few that would be "the perfect leadership mixture," yet so much of that varies from person to person and situation to situation.

I see the attributes, skills, and behaviors that I present here as making a difference to people I work with and for and have researched and observed over the years within leadership roles. Some are similar to what you may have read in other books and are proven by decades of research. Some are based solely on my practice in what I see making a difference and even getting frustrated with people and shouting, "You can't be such an asshole if you want to be a leader!" Or even, "You need to be more of an asshole to better position yourself and purpose!"

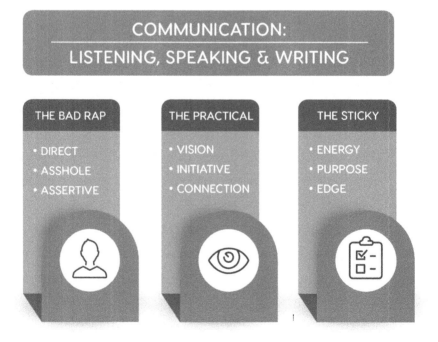

I look at several different attributes, skills, and behaviors here. Don't try to practice each one right away. Pick and choose which one, or ones, would work best for you now and within your realm of practice and decisions. Regardless of the various attributes, skills, and behaviors I list here, what matters to you, as a person and as a leader outside of this text, are the attributes, skills, and behaviors that will enable you to better lead and make a difference in your own life with the value you bring, your purpose, and your decisions.

Disregard the broad-based skills that leadership experts tell you to worry about. Concentrate on the ones that matter to you and for your own life. You can learn more about what those are in getting feedback through evaluation along with extending your awareness as part of the A/P/E Model.

11

Communication

One essential skill that I hear people talk about for strong leaders is communication. Could anything be more vague and unhelpful than saying that communication is the key to great leadership? What does that even mean? I hear this a lot when talking to clients looking for training for their teams or themselves. They start the conversation by saying, "I need a course on communication. It needs to improve, and it needs to improve now!"

When hearing this, I laugh (to myself) and then begin to dig into what's really happening. What's the deeper issue that makes them think the problem is communication? Sometimes the answer is in being clearer in articulating what they want or in creating and delivering better presentations, which can be more individually based than team based. Before looking at communication as it relates to leadership, let's look at communication itself keeping in mind that this is not a book specifically about communication; it's a book about how you make decisions that enable you to lead.

We can think about how we can make better decisions and how we communicate. Let's define what this means to you first, similar to what we did with defining leadership. When you even hear the word *communication*, what comes to mind? Most likely you have several words, pictures, and behaviors that you associate with communication springing to your brain. You could be thinking about writing emails, letters, texts, tweets, white papers, infographics, memos, research papers, speeches, scripts, flyers, and newsletters to name a few mediums. You may think about communication concerning speech or audio. You're thinking about conversations, meetings, presentations, videos, FaceTime, conference calls, and webinars.

Let's look at communication here from three viewpoints in how we make our leadership decisions. Those include

▶ Listening

▶ Speaking

▶ Writing

Did you list listening as a form of communication? Maybe you did. Not many of us are good listeners. We did not grow up learning how to listen. But listening is so essential to leadership in wanting to connect with others. Let's first look at how we decide to listen to others, and what this skill can do to enhance our Leadership Brand and our Leadership Lifestyle.

Listening

When I was conducting research for my doctorate, I was talking to a midlevel leader at a university medical center where she was enrolled in a leadership development program. We were discussing the program, which she found to be of great value to her in her current role and to her life overall in how she led. From this interview, I recall the words she said, "Learning leadership has helped me at work, at home, and church." The church mention, at the time, was shocking to me. Why? Remember, leadership is a lifestyle and not just a title at work meaning that it applies to *all* aspects of life: work, religion, home, and so forth. We'll continue to talk about this, but her addressing religion caught my attention and made me listen to her further. I was intrigued.

When talking about what she was learning within the leadership development program, she noted how she was learning to become a better communicator and discussed improving her skills when presenting and writing. I agreed that communication was an essential skill for leaders to have and tried to push her on to the next question so I could move on with my day. She stopped me and said something I'll never forget. She said that not only is communication writing and speaking, but it's also about listening. I felt like she read my mind and knew I was checking out of the interview even with my intrigue about her church comment. I was speechless. Now I was really listening.

She further explained that one of the biggest takeaways from the program was that leaders must listen and must listen well to ensure effectiveness through connection. Think about when you were in school—elementary, middle, high school, college, and beyond. Most likely, you've taken class after class on how to write essays and how to give effective presentations. When did you ever take a class on how to listen? If you're like most, you haven't. I ask this when teaching courses about feedback and how essential listening is to giving and receiving feedback as part of an evaluation. A few students will raise their hands, and mostly those who attended schools outside of the United States, but most have not.

When I gave my TEDx Talk in 2013, I spoke about the importance of listening as an essential yet unsung skill that leaders should possess. We never really take time to learn how to be good listeners. Of course, that theory was challenged by some via the YouTube page that the recording is hosted on saying that to do well in school you learn how to listen well and use those skills through social interactions. If that is the case, then why isn't it taught as a formal skill for school success, let alone for leadership success? Can you imagine the impact that a listening class would have on people at a young age?

The only time I recall ever taking a listening lesson was in fifth grade. We had to sit across from a peer who had to tell us a story, about anything, for one minute. We had to focus on them as they spoke and couldn't break eye contact. Post-story, we were told to ask three questions as a follow-up and then make three observations about their story and how they told it. That's the only time I recall taking a class, or lesson, about listening. I shredded my pencil along the ring of my binder trying to complete this exercise as I found it so difficult.

No doubt at some point in your life you've felt that someone hasn't listened to you. Maybe a friend or a partner. That feeling is infuriating. It can make us feel helpless and worthless. When someone doesn't value you enough to put the phone down and listen, where you feel as if they are not truly listening and focusing on you, it can change your perspective about them and doubt your relationship with them.

You may have experienced this circumstance from a personal perspective at some point in life, but you may also have experienced a leader who hasn't listened. By not listening to you, let's suppose that this leader made some mistake or a poor move. In experiencing that, you could have thought further about your listening skills and worked on shutting the laptop during meetings, turning the Skype off during one-on-one touch bases, and writing notes when you hear people speaking and repeating what they say back to you.

Those are common practices when thinking about listening or trying to improve your ability. Listening helps us hear what's being said through words, tone, and body language. It helps us value the person and the relationship. It helps us gain awareness in understanding someone else's perspective so we can better connect and use this knowledge to make better decisions both in advancing what we are trying to do in being more effective as leaders.

Listening is a decision like everything else we've discussed. We can decide to listen, or not. We can decide to value people, or not. We can choose to make this part of practice, or not. So think to yourself: are you listening? If you are unsure, this can be a valuable and first place to get feedback from those who experience you and how they perceive your Leadership Brand.

Speaking

As leaders, we need to use our voice to communicate our decisions, to deliver our value, to challenge and encourage perceptions of those around us to view us as leaders, and to get people to trust us and our leadership ability. Having a voice and being able to use it to our benefit is vital if we want people to connect with us, understand our purpose, and realize and act upon our vision.

We want leaders who are articulate, clear, and decisive when they speak. The most essential leadership skill (and the one I frequently hear) is the importance of leaders being good public speakers. Earlier I talked about public speaking and leadership in thinking about perception is reality in that we can perceive and experience an excellent public speaker from that of someone who needs to improve.

Does being an excellent public speaker always equate with strong leadership? Do we need to be good at public speaking to be a good leader? To me, good public speaking matters to a point. From a perception and value standpoint, we aren't going to trust someone who can't get a sentence out in front of a group of people. We'd question their vision. We'd question their confidence. In questioning both, we'd doubt their value as a leader.

However, all leaders don't need to be TED-Talk-worthy speakers. They may stumble over a word or two. That's being human. That's being vulnerable. As leaders, whatever our mission is, we need to have a voice. Sometimes the best speakers can be the worst leaders. Charisma can only get us so far. And sometimes that gets into a gray area when we define strong leadership in terms of those who speak well publicly with those who truly have great ideas, purpose, and initiative. Recognize that real leaders may falter.

Observe those people you define and perceive value in as leaders. Watch how they talk. You may notice patterns. Not all will be the best public speakers, but notice what you value about the way that they communicate vocally. I often see the best ones being direct and clear in their delivery. They have an easy way of sharing what their vision is. There's also a level of honesty about whether they know something or have made a mistake. I also feel a level of connectedness in the way that they deliver their messages whether it is through eye contact, inflection, or humility. Those in formal leadership roles who struggle may do so for many reasons and all of which could be quickly addressed in deciding to improve their ability to communicate verbally regardless of where they are in their career.

I worked with one leader, Liz, and would often wonder how she got to such a high level within the organization. Among other flaws, her communication skills were awful as she lacked clarity, direction, and confidence when she spoke both one-on-one and in team meetings or to larger groups. She never made consistent eye contact. She never spoke with confidence. She was never clear in her asks. She interrupted people when they spoke. She made comments at the wrong times that showed she wasn't present or listening. Liz never clearly articulated a vision for the future and how each one of those people on this team played an integral part.

All of these behaviors, whether conscious or not, demonstrated a level of decision-making on her part as a leader as she wasn't positioning himself to be perceived as one based on these behaviors and her overall lack of awareness. Not only is public speaking essential but being able to communicate to others in the hall, over coffee, and in meetings is equally crucial. I don't think that every leader needs to be a perfect speaker. It does come down to the awareness of who needs to know what and then communicating that message to them.

Are you using both the A/P/E Model and TOLL to make better decisions about the ways that you talk in the public speaking setting, in general meetings, or one-on-one? How are you making decisions about the way that you use your voice as it relates to your leadership in the day-to-day and to the overall legacy and mission of your Leadership Brand? Out of all the aspects of communication, decide to focus on this and to focus on this now. How are you deciding to communicate your brand every day as it relates to your brand, as it relates to perception, and as it impacts your decisions? While this may be daunting in asks, if people can't follow what you say, you will not be leading.

Writing

Written communication takes a variety of forms. We text. We email. We use messaging platforms. It's relentless in how we must write as leaders and deliver messages. I've had some leaders say, "Don't text me!" while some say, "Text me anytime" in order to show support. Some send texts or messages that are well-written, clear, and helpful. Others send slang and undecipherable texts that make you wonder if they had been drinking when sending.

We don't need to have perfect grammar, or spelling, to be effective in written communication, but we do need to consider how we present our Leadership Brand in how we communicate when we write. Some people get more hung up on this than others in trying to find value in others. It's not simply the text, it's the bigger purpose and message that we should concern ourselves with more. Are we clear and concise, or sloppy and vague? We can use our Feedback Board, Success Team, and those with experience to get feedback on how we can be more effective in how we write and take the initiative to make better decisions in using this medium in demonstrating our value.

Let's specifically look at email, as I hear people judge leaders frequently on this medium. Yet, no one ever said and meant, "That person is a great leader since they write great emails." Sometimes the most useful emails can be just a few words to get the point across. But we could position it more along the lines of, "I understand what this person is saying to me in terms of action and vision in a clear and concise way." Basically, "I know what to do and why" because the email is direct in communicating a vision and a purpose.

If improving your written communication is where you want to focus your leadership decisions, it's a good decision to make. Let's look at the simple steps and communication mediums that can help set your thinking for the bigger picture of leadership communication. Say your goal is "to write better emails" as you think this will make you sound more authoritative when communicating to people, both individuals and groups based on feedback you've received. But what makes a well-written email? Language choice? Facts? Length?

Do you know someone who writes emails that you admire? Consider what you find helpful about those emails. Talk to them about how they write and what their process looks like. Also consider if this person should be part of your Success Team or Feedback Board. Along with adding this person to your team, make this process easier on yourself in creating "cheat sheets" of templates to use. Practice writing. Read more books, newsletters, or blogs written by people similar to your style to get a further feel on how thought leaders talk. Listen to webinars. Work on your listening during meetings and reflect what you hear in taking notes to test what you heard and how you rephrase.

These are just a sampling of a few ways that you can begin to improve your email writing ability if this is something that you find as a challenge as a leader and feel it would make a difference to you. These are all decisions in gaining awareness, practicing something new, and evaluating your work with the help of others. In thinking about this awareness and in inviting people to be a part of your leadership Success Team and Feedback Board, you now have people who can aid you during your practice and evaluation phase of the A/P/E Model.

Summary

Communication is important to leadership. Saying leaders are effective communicators is not enough, though, as we need to understand what that means to us and why when we look to define value in people in leadership roles. At the start of this chapter, I explained that this is not a book about communication. There are hundreds of books, courses, eLearning offerings, webinars, blogs, and the like that focus on communication and every medium of communication. Much of this content is flawlessly written, spoken to, and shared. Consume as much of it as you possibly can if you need to get better in this area.

Don't lose yourself in it, or use communication as a broader umbrella for more specific areas of development. Think to yourself: What matters to me? What matters most to the people I would lead? What do my advisors tell me is most important to improve? What can I make decisions about and why does this matter to my leadership and what I'm trying to accomplish?

Make that decision about how you want to improve as a communicator and why. Why is that particular thread of the communication weave essential to your leadership development? Know that within that weave there are some components of communication that matter more to some leaders and certain situations than others. It's not enough just to say that leaders are good communicators and to be a better leader you need to be a better communicator. It's not that simple, and it's not that hard. You can practice communication and what you define to be of most value to your leadership ability.

You can then work to evaluate the improvements that you've made based on reading your work and turning to members of your Success Team for help. You can decide on enhancing communication via all elements of the A/P/E Model. The simplest way that I can define strong leadership communication is being aware of who needs to know what, why they do, and then ensuring they get the message. That's a decision. Furthermore, consider this outline:

- ▸ Awareness
  - How do you define leadership's value as it relates to communication in listening, writing, and speaking?
  - What communication skills are perceived as most important by those around you whether at home, work, or school? How do you know that?

- What communication skills are your strengths? Weaknesses?

▶ Practice
- What communication skills can you decide to practice improving on now and how?
- What communication skills can you decide to continue to do well with and how?
- How can you decide to practice improved communication in all aspects of your Leadership Lifestyle?

▶ Evaluation
- What formal methods as part of your Leadership Lifestyle can you use to gain evaluation on your communication skills—both strengths and weaknesses?
- How can you use your Feedback Team and Success Board to gain evaluation and feedback on your practice?
- How can you self-evaluate your communication efforts as part of your Leadership Lifestyle? What is making a difference? How do you know?

Let's now transition to looking at leadership attributes, behaviors, and skills as they align to the A/P/E acronym of the A/P/E Model. In developing those attributes and behaviors presented, we can determine what makes the most sense for us to practice in using the A/P/E Model.

12

The Bad Rap

Let's first look at some of the leadership attributes that have a bad rap. Those addressed include being direct, not being an asshole (not being one or maybe being one when you need to), and being assertive. These attributes impact those around us and help us to be influential leaders. These attributes help us work better with people and dictate the perceptions of others about us—yet can sometimes be misinterpreted if we don't communicate properly how we see these benefiting ourselves as leaders and those we lead.

Direct

I like people who are direct. Those who are clear and easy to understand what they want so it makes it easier to follow them and understand their vision. Those who give honest feedback to help you or a team or project realign. Being direct isn't a bad thing, although sometimes people consider it an unlikable attribute. Yet, if we don't know what our leaders want, or as leaders we're not simply communicating to others what we want or where we see them lacking or following through, we won't be effective.

This lack of directness can be a point of frustration for both leaders and their followers when there is no direction of what the overall vision is. Vision is an attribute that I'll talk about later, but one that's essential in how being direct and clear dictates the success of a vision coming to life. Even if we have that vision, we need to ensure others know what their part of it is so they can take action. This can take practice in trying to communicate to others in a more direct way than what we are used to or comfortable with. Trying to be more direct is also a skill you want to communicate to others who are trying so they understand why you are trying to change and what it will achieve.

I've sat in meetings with leaders who talk and talk and talk to share their vision and their thoughts. Yet, at the end of the meeting, people walk out not knowing what's expected by whom and by when. Nothing happens since no one knows where to start. The next meeting, there's nothing to regroup on, and the leader is frustrated that their team didn't do anything. In being direct, we clarify what we want and what our expectations are. Being direct also enables us to give clear and actionable feedback to those we lead.

Start asking for feedback using the A/P/E Model in considering evaluation and getting feedback on how people understand your vision and your expectations of those around you. You may think you are being clear, at points, but find yourself getting frustrated when no action has been taken. With this awareness, we can begin to be more direct and see the results that occur because of it. Being direct doesn't mean being rude or cruel to people in a way that's hurtful, which is where it may get a bad reputation. It does challenge us to consider how we communicate to others so they know where to act, which can aid our Leadership Brand in people being able to trust and follow us as leaders due to this level of transparency.

Asshole

Being an asshole is a debatable leadership behavior. No other leadership text is going to tell you this. No research is going to answer the question, "To what extent does a leader need to be an asshole to be effective?" We can look at this behavior in two ways. The first being we don't need to be an asshole to be effective in being disrespectful to people or treating them poorly. Gaining a leadership role within an organization does not give you a right to be an asshole. Second, sometimes we need to be an asshole to get things done or assert ourselves and our vision.

I worked for Julian, who was an asshole. He ripped people down by criticizing them publicly, he would scream in people's faces when they made a mistake, and he would talk crap to his team members about one another. People hated him yet pitied him at the same time. Because of his behavior, people left to find better jobs where they weren't treated so poorly. Those who knew him knew his Leadership Brand and his pattern of treating people like this, so when Julian was fired from the job and needed help, no one would help him.

Don't make decisions that make you look like an asshole as they demonstrate how you lack compassion and empathy along with overall awareness. If you do, don't ever be that asshole who can't apologize or admit wrong. We admire the leaders who can be vulnerable (remember that even CEOs get diarrhea). We respect leaders who treat people like people. We as leaders should treat people like people.

People like Julian are not leaders. They are bullies in leadership roles. If you are currently working for someone you think is an asshole like Julian, leave. You are only hurting yourself by reporting to and working for someone that you think is an asshole. If you think you are like Julian, I encourage you to take some time to self-assess why you may equate leadership with being a bully and use the A/P/E Model to explore this further.

As leaders, we can't be walked all over either. Sometimes we may need to be an asshole. Maybe that means taking a tough stand for the right decision or an unpopular one— whether being tested by others and requiring us to take a stand, hitting hard in a negotiation, or standing up for someone on your team or someone you care about.

A friend of mine, Abby, once felt like she was being an asshole during a work project. No one was listening to her, or so she felt. One man on her project team stood up to assert himself when she was talking and she lost her mind. She slammed her hand on the table and raised her voice and said she wanted to be heard and that no one in the room was listening to her. She wanted to know why. They all sat blankly and looked at her.

Abby continued on with the meeting and knew, moving forward, she'd have to be more assertive and tough in order to get things done with this group, but felt like she needed to be an asshole to do it. It was uncomfortable for her, but that was a pivotal moment as the team progressed and ended the project with huge success. She told me after about this and how uncomfortable she was and how she felt like an asshole, but without that stand and being assertive, the team's work under her leadership would have failed.

Sometimes we may need to be comfortable as leaders in voicing our opinions or being tough with those we work with to drive results. We may even need to be that asshole to assert our Leadership Brand and vision to people. But we need to be mindful to not be an asshole to treat people poorly because we think we can as a leader or align that with the idea of power or strength. It's not. It's knowing when to use our decisions to position us in a way that shows strength without being degrading.

Assertive

I worked with a VP named Will who moved up the ranks somewhat quickly, yet Will never had any opinion one way or the other or showed any emotion. He never got mad. He never seemed happy. He never pushed any of his opinions. He was just kind of … there. People found him hard to connect to and thought he was unconfident because he lacked assertion.

Will gained feedback on this from his peers and from Leslie, his manager who was an executive, as part of the performance management cycle. Part of Will's plan to become a better leader was to work on his assertiveness if he wanted to move up formally. As much as Leslie valued him, she knew that Will wouldn't be the right fit for the role if he didn't practice his assertiveness and make a decision to do so. Leslie informed Will that being an executive meant that he needed to be assertive and confident in talking to the other executive team members who had mastered this skill.

In gaining this awareness while practicing communicating to enhance his Leadership Brand, Will made an effort to practice being assertive. In meetings, he practiced voicing his opinion. He worked on speaking up overall and saying no and sharing his thoughts on why. Over time, the perceptions about Will's leadership started changing as he began to vocalize further. The feedback changed, and his peers, teams, and Leslie noticed that once he became more assertive, he became more confident. He started to look like an executive. Leslie now talks about Will eventually taking her place when the time comes.

Leaders need to be assertive and, as a subset of this, confident. We need our leaders to have an opinion, to say yes or no. We need to feel comfortable that they will speak up when needed and be confident enough to do so. Deciding to be a leader is a decision and act of assertion. Being assertive gives direction to those we lead. It gives us faith that our leaders have confidence and know which direction to move in. As leaders, we also need this to feel the strength in the decisions we make about what we do. We also need this direction to motivate and inspire those around us. Don't confuse overconfidence and cockiness with assertiveness. You can be assertive without being an asshole too.

Everyone has a point of view. People have opinions. People have emotions. People know what they want. Sharing those is what helps us connect and establish who we are as leaders and what our Leadership Brand is. Assertion and expressing that enables us to do so. It can be hard to practice, for some, but essential if we want to improve our leadership ability.

13

The Practical

The practical behaviors and attributes of leadership that I outline here ask you to think about the basics of how you will lead and influence those around you through vision, initiative, and connection. I call these practical as they are the foundational attributes and behaviors that you will base your leadership decisions on. Not only will these attributes guide you within the professional setting, but they will also aid in how you define your Leadership Brand and live your Leadership Lifestyle.

Vision

Part of leadership is knowing what you want to do and how you plan to do it. Simply, having a vision. Later on, we'll examine purpose, which overlaps with vision. I've often heard that people say leaders are strategic, which we can somewhat align with vision from the angle of having a plan.

Our visions as leaders stem from deciding to unite our purpose with our actions and behavior to reach a particular goal. That's leading.

Without a vision that's then driven by our decisions about initiative, purpose, and awareness, people will struggle to follow us in what we are trying to achieve. People often associate leadership with that of the function of the people manager in the corporate world, to be a leader, one must have people to lead, even if it is only managing the ins and outs of the business. A vision defines leadership whether you lead people formally or not.

We can have all the vision in the world, but if we aren't making decisions to communicate that vision and use it to motivate others and take initiative to act, we fail in leading. Having a vision gives us a map to lead and inspire those around us. Imagine trying to follow someone without a plan. What would that look like or feel like? Sometimes, when I think about leadership and leaders, I think about mountains. When I interact with those in leadership roles at work, I think to myself:

▶ Would I follow this person up a mountain outside of work?

▶ Do they care about my well-being in climbing that mountain?

▶ Do they have a plan to climb the mountain in a way that makes sense?

This so-called leader may have no formal mountain climbing experience, and that isn't what matters. What matters is being able to say, "Yes, I'd follow this person up a mountain since they're a great leader with a plan and they care about me," or "No. Heck no. I'd never follow this person up a mountain. They don't plan (or have a vision), and they don't care."

Next time you meet someone who's a leader, ask yourself: Would you climb the mountain with that person? Do you trust their plan in climbing? Think about the planning you do, or don't do. Would you climb a mountain with someone like you in a leadership role? Second, consider if you are communicating your vision to those around you in a way that enables them to make decisions on how and where they can act.

Initiative

In the way I define leadership, I place emphasis on initiative as you may have noticed throughout reading. I think about a story I heard in a class I taught once. In my class, we were talking about leading organizational change. George raised his hand to share a story about a leader he works for who fails at leading change and describes Monday mornings at the office. George is in his early fifties and works at a pharmaceutical company. Every Monday, his boss, Tony, comes in with a new idea for change.

Tony's staff, and George particularly, have become very annoyed at this weekly habit, and less than optimistic that any changes Tony announces on Monday will ever have any life after that day. George and his colleagues have change burnout since every week it's something new, yet nothing ever changes. George admits that Tony had good intentions in coming into work every Monday wanting to make a difference. But nothing was ever done. Every week, it was the same thing.

Tony took no true initiative or action, he simply just talked about his vision. Earlier on, we talked about how we've overglorified and overcomplicated leadership. We want our leaders to be capable and have desirable skills. In reading this, we should want the same for ourselves.

Good leaders and the way they lead can be summed up to many things, but one thing that we may lose track of is that good leaders are also practical in that they take action. They do. Leaders need to take initiative to be effective. There's nothing wrong with initiative. Think about the opposite. Think about George's boss who wants to make a change every week. Is that practical? Is that taking initiative? No. George and his peers were annoyed with Tony since he never acted on his vision or ideas. He only talked.

Maybe Tony spent the weekends trying to educate himself and to make better decisions about his leadership so that when he came to work on Monday, he was excited to make a change based on his increased awareness and desire to practice what he thought he needed in order to lead. But he lacked initiative to practice. It takes the decision every day and the initiative every day to make things happen, to change things, to, well, really lead.

This may be the biggest challenge holding you back from truly leading. Maybe you are fearful, or maybe you don't know where to start. Whatever the case may be, you need to find a way to act. That is how you lead and that is the biggest and hardest decision to make.

Connection

People ask me about emotional intelligence when I instruct leadership courses. Some people don't care about this level of humanness while some care tremendously. While we should consider what emotional intelligence looks like to us, as leaders, we should further define how comfortable we are with this and what those around us need from us in this realm. Many can agree that emotions are needed to lead. We all have emotions, and we all vary in how much we show on a regular basis and to whom. While I agree that these are important topics that are heavily researched and written about, I want to focus more on the practicality of connection in this section.

Earlier, I talked about Suzanne, who told me people didn't like me, and the struggles I had with her as my manager. In that same conversation, Suzanne told me that I was hard to connect with, which was another reason I'd never be promoted, which hurt me incredibly. But I felt that way about her as a leader. There had been times she'd shown me empathy if someone passed away or if deadlines were tough, but none of that mattered since I never felt connected to her, her visions, or her leadership.

You don't have to always like someone or show empathy to feel connected, but if someone sees what you are doing and why, they can find their own ways to connect to it for their own reasons.

We see this with political leaders all the time. They talk about how they feel or show empathy via some wording in a speech or how they present themselves, but we connect with their vision and how they communicate that as part of their Leadership Brand and Leadership Lifestyle from what we know about them. They make decisions and create visions that we can relate to and feel connected to that make us feel part of something. We want our leaders to make us feel part of something. As leaders, we are leading people. We aren't leading computers. We aren't leading fire ants. We aren't leading Excel. People need to feel connected.

Think about how you are connecting as a tool to aid in your leadership and how you can further use your decisions to maximize your connections to your benefit. Emotions and emotional connections are important for leaders in forming relationships and empathy. That works for some and not others as not all leaders feel comfortable showing emotions, yet all leaders need to find ways to connect.

14

The Sticky

It's time to talk about a topic that some will love, and others will hate—further defining your Leadership Brand as it deals with the intangible and the "sticky." This chapter focuses on the attributes and behaviors that stick with us throughout our lives and careers when we think about how those we followed led and how they made us feel. I define the sticky as having energy, purpose, and edge.

These are the sticky attributes that give you more insight on areas that you may not have given thought to previously about yourself as a leader and as a person leading a Leadership Lifestyle through your decisions. You may not agree with these attributes as being sticky, but challenge yourself to consider what makes leaders stand out in your mind, similar to how we defined leadership earlier on. What are those hard-to-define yet noticeable behaviors and attributes that make some leaders hard to forget?

Energy

We feed off the energy of others. If we are out with friends and one is feeling blue, it may affect the mood of the night. If we have a team member who hates their job, we feel it. Our perceptions about leaders are formed by the energy we feel from them. In looking deeper, we need to be connected to ourselves in thinking about how we interact with those around us and how we do this through our level of energy. If we're enthusiastic about something, we have that passion. Passion about a particular topic, project, or job. It excites us. Others feel it.

I think about Marji and Janet when I think about energy when it comes to leadership. Marji produces healthcare conferences specifically on Medicare. She's midtwenties, educated, and driven. For most, the topic of Medicare is less than thrilling. But to Marji, Medicare is life. When she explained what she was creating for a Medicare conference agenda, her face would light up. She would outline Medicare like she was talking about her childhood crush. It made others on her team get excited, too, about Medicare.

Her conferences did exceptionally well from the standpoint of attendee feedback, revenue, and longevity. Now, over a decade later, she still comes to mind for me when I think about energy due to the passion she had for the topic. It made her sticky as a leader since people wanted to feel what she felt too.

On the opposite side of that, my heart sinks as I think about Janet. Janet had a great job in marketing and said it was her passion. She had been in marketing for years, and her resume was a masterpiece of all her accomplishments and a demonstration of her marketing leadership. But working was hell. She complained all the time about the leaders above her, about the work she had to do, and how much she hated coming in every day.

Prior to Janet coming on board, I had been happy in my role. But her constant complaining, whining, and negative comments brought me down. I lost my own passion for the role and my energy took a dip. I worked less, put in half the effort when I was there, and felt myself developing an attitude. Others noticed too.

Once Janet left the company, I felt my spirits lift and my anxiety release. It made me realize how her toxicity was damaging my mental health and the decisions I was making about my role and about my career. I began to lose passion due to her energy.

Maybe you have something you're passionate about. Maybe you don't and are still trying to figure that out. Regardless of what that looks like to you, as leaders we need to make decisions about how we use our energy to impact and excite ourselves and those we lead. We can reframe it as, "How can I get others excited about what I'm doing as a leader?"

In the example with Marji, she was thrilled to talk about Medicare. Her passion was so electric that it excited those around her based on her enthusiasm, unlike Janet's lack of awareness about how her unhappiness impacted those around her.

Energy gets us excited to go to work and work for leaders who care. When we see leaders get excited about something, it helps us connect to them matched with their vision and purpose. We can use our decisions and our mindset to build excitement in what we do and why and use that as a tool to excite others around us. Being able to use our energy to build ourselves and others helps us stick as leaders.

Purpose

When deciding to lead, along with defining leadership for us and its value to our decisions, we need to clarify our purpose. Considering questions like what are we trying to do and why. Why does this matter to others? What action do I need to take to translate my purpose into vision to then act and lead?

Our purpose gives us passion like Marji. Our purpose gives us drive to take initiative. Our purpose provides us with the motivation to lead and to influence others. It's the map by which we plot our leadership and influence those around us. Purpose gives us energy to lead. Purpose, though, can be tricky. It's like asking that high school senior what they want to be when they grow up. Sometimes, we don't know. That's okay. Not having some big plan or strategy is okay. It can take time to figure out. Even the purpose of saying, "Today I want to be a better leader, and I'm going to make one decision today to reach that goal," is a step in the right direction. It's a step closer to finding our purpose and living the Leadership Lifestyle based on our decisions.

Maybe at work, we don't see opportunities to lead, but outside of work, we see a need to create a networking group to help people in our community. Here, we can find a purpose in seeking opportunity. Here, we can find ways to practice and make decisions about our leadership. Think about the people you consider to be leaders. They all have a purpose. They all have a story in which to lead by and to develop their Leadership Brand's foundation. In having that they find ways to draw you into that purpose. It's like magic.

I worked with a woman named Anne who could do this as she felt marketing was her life. A simple task or project would be turned into your calling in the way she'd speak about its implications and your importance to it for our clients. She saw purpose in everything she did when it came to marketing and found ways through storytelling and connecting that made others feel the same. People are drawn to purpose. People were drawn to Anne and wanted to work for her because she felt so passionately about her purpose in working in marketing and the impact it made. We want something to work toward, to find value in, and to bond ourselves with others.

As leaders, we can give this thought as we make decisions about what our purpose is and how we can live our purpose through our decisions and our Leadership Lifestyle. Finding your purpose may be easier said than done. Take time to think about this and how it aligns with your leadership so you can begin to map the difference you want to make. It creates the foundation for your Leadership Brand, while giving you something to strive for. Purpose gives us something to lead by.

Edge

I worked with Chris who talked about edge and its importance to leaders. Edge was never an attribute that I had heard about after all the leadership courses I had taken, books I had read, and research I had done. Chris would talk about how edge separated the leaders with a backbone from those who were in the formality of a role and spineless. I never had thought of it before, but once I began to consider what edge looked like, I saw it in leaders around me. I saw it in leaders whom I had worked for and with historically. They were the people whom I knew were leaders but couldn't quite put my finger on what made them so special but they stuck out in my mind.

Edge is a sticky skill in knowing how to use it to your benefit without seeming rebellious or rogue. Edge requires us to have confidence. Edge is that tone of voice to prove a point spoken at the right time to make an impact. Edge is the willingness to take a risk. Edge is speaking up when you may challenge popular opinion, but know you need to in order to stay true to your Leadership Brand. It can be compassion in doing the right thing or rebellious in knowing when to take a chance.

Having an edge or being edgy isn't a bad thing. It shouldn't be considered as one although sometimes it may be by some if misunderstood. Edge isn't loud or angry, but it is decisive and strong. Having an edge gives us a presence and clout to our Leadership Brand. It makes people remember us as leaders.

Plus, edge can give us a way to connect. Ever speak up in a meeting and then have people whom you never talk to approach you after and say that you said what was on their mind but they were afraid to say it? Maybe you never talked to them before, but when you took the risk, you were able to connect and maybe make a bigger difference. You were saying the words that were in your peers' minds that they were too scared to say themselves.

This is a decision. It's a decision we can make when we decide to speak up or stay silent. We can decide to fight or not to fight. To get dirty or stay clean. Edge can give us the upper hand to cut through the tape, or the crap, and make an actual difference when leading and inspiring others. Edge may look different to you and it may be a hard attribute to master and master well.

15

Aligning the Behaviors and Skills to Your Decisions and the A/P/E Model

When I think about the A/P/E Model and TOLL in action, I think about a man named Ronald. He took classes both at work and outside of work to expand his awareness about leadership. He practiced what he learned. He asked his teams, family, and friends for feedback on what he was doing and how those around him perceived his decisions and his initiative.

Ronald thought about the timing of his life, overall, and when it made the most sense for him to make bigger decisions in relation to his leadership. He sought out opportunities both inside and outside of work to stretch and challenge himself as a leader. He also cared how he felt as a leader. Ronald took great care in building relationships with his team and working on himself so he felt a sense of "like" in all matters. From these decisions, he grew as a person and as a leader.

In the previous chapter, I outlined several attributes, behaviors, and skills to consider in thinking about how you can make decisions about your leadership. Books, articles, experts, and the like have different views on the skills that make a leader, a leader, and that's where the awareness part of the A/P/E Model helps. But the A/P/E Model pushes us to take action toward making decisions that will propel us into true leaders.

In working with the different elements of the cycle, you gain awareness by practicing and evaluating. You need to give thought to what skills and behaviors make sense for you in your life and in being a leader. What makes sense for you to work on that would enable you to lead? In knowing that, how can you use the A/P/E Model to make further decisions to enhance your leadership? Those are what you should be practicing. You can seek this awareness through the mediums that I outlined in the awareness section. Ask the people around you. Ask your Feedback and Success teams. Survey those you work with. Whatever makes sense for you, decide to do it.

Once you are practicing and evaluating, you can make further decisions on how you can apply leadership skills and behaviors in your life. That's the essence of the A/P/E Model. It's flexible with what you need in your life. It merely encourages you to make decisions to do so while also providing you with new ideas on what could make a difference to you.

I talk and consult with so many people who feel stuck when it comes to their leadership. They feel like they need to be perfect. They feel like once they are promoted, they are officially a leader in the work sense. It's frustrating to hear this as it demonstrates to me that they don't understand what leadership is. You are, or are not, a leader whether you have the title or not.

Many organizations further justify people getting promoted, as the managers want those people to be acting as leaders before they formally grant a title via a promotion. Other leadership experts will argue that the most natural of leaders will be leading whether they have the role or not. That's the sign of a true leader—the ability to lead without a title. That's what you should be focused on as the goal of your Leadership Lifestyle.

When or if you receive that promotion doesn't mean that the journey is over. It's still a work in progress. It's always a daily decision in the way that we live our lives. If you are a leader now in the formal work sense, it also doesn't mean that your journey is over. You need to continually be working on yourself to be a leader and to improve on being a leader.

Leadership is not a check-the-box activity. Leadership is a decision that's reflected in the A/P/E Model and within our Leadership Lifestyle. Throughout this section, for each behavior and skill, we tied back to the application of using the A/P/E Model to make decisions about each. These behaviors and skills also relate to TOLL.

As discussed earlier, the A/P/E Model can aid in your overall decision-making about your leadership, but TOLL offers a different lens to make decisions. The elements of TOLL, similar to that of the A/P/E Model, can also be tied back to the leadership behaviors and skills outlined.

Now that we've further developed our understanding about leadership and discovered how the A/P/E Model can aid in making decisions about our leadership, and addressed skills and behaviors that can enhance our leadership practice, let's move forward to the final part. In this concluding material, I give further consideration to what you may do once completing this book and moving forward with making decisions as part of your Leadership Lifestyle.

As you move forward and gain further awareness about your timing and opportunity, ask yourself these questions:

▶ What can I use now to make decisions about my Leadership Lifestyle?

▶ Whom can I begin using as part of my Feedback Team and Success Board to gain immediate evaluation to aid in the initial steps of the awareness stage?

▸ Where and how can I create opportunity immediately to begin practicing my leadership decisions through my behaviors and skills?

The final chapter focuses on the practicality of what you need to do now to define your leadership path moving forward based on understanding the A/P/E Model and TOLL in making decisions about your leadership.

PART IV:

Now What?

"The only person you are destined to become is
the person you decide to be."
Ralph Waldo Emerson

16

Will You Decide to Lead Today?

You've made it. You've finished the book. Now what? Well, that's up to you. You may see leaders where you didn't see leaders before. You could now see the truth that some people in leadership roles are not leaders, just people with fancy titles. You now realize the power you have to make decisions about your Leadership Brand with the use of the A/P/E Model.

With the A/P/E Model, you've gained awareness. You've increased awareness about yourself and the attributes, skills, and behaviors that contemporary leaders need to be successful. You've explored ways to practice your leadership ability and how to evaluate your practice, your growth, and your ability.

Taking a step back and finding time to evaluate can aid in your overall growth by helping you see improvements through your practice and the perceptions of others. Trust in yourself and in the work you put into this. It will pay off. When you begin to feel frustrated that things aren't going the way you think they should, or you come up against challenges that are larger than you, remember TOLL.

Remembering that *timing* and *opportunity* are a part of the journey can help in relaxing qualms about your leadership development. Timing and opportunity can help as a guide for looking at your current situation. What can you change? What can't be changed? What is this telling you about what you need to do?

As soon as you chose to read this book, you made a decision about your leadership. You made a decision like you do each day about aspects of your life. You took the initiative to read and to finish it. You now can decide to lead and make decisions on how you will, and how you can, do this. Decide now to make a difference. Decide now to think about your behaviors in regard to your situation and your life.

Will you decide to lead today?

Acknowledgments

My parents always told me, "Make the right decisions." They said it when I'd leave the house, when I'd go to bed, and anytime they could. I like to think I did. Thank you, Mary and James Rymsha.

Thanks to my aunts, Elaine Drolet and Anne Hession, for their constant support, grit, and humor. Both have shared their own stories of leadership that have made me laugh and cringe.

My friends have given me honest feedback throughout my life both on personal and professional issues. These people have shared beers, given me support, and listened to me when I needed it. Specifically, I'd like to thank Alison McGonagle-O'Connell, Sean Fielding, Tom Donovan, and Natalia Vudvud.

Notes

Introduction

Leadership has grown in popularity. Chris Westfall, "Leadership development is a $366 billion industry: here's why most programs don't work," *Forbes*, June 21, 2019.

Chapter 1

I can't stop thinking about our company meeting yesterday. Kristine Buonopane (Dunn), LinkedIn comment. Viewed April 6, 2017.

The average CEO age is fifty-six, and the average CFO and COO age is fifty-two. WorldatWork.com, "Average age for C-suite member is 56," January 20, 2020.

Only 19 percent of US congressional members, less than 5 percent of Fortune 500 CEOs, and only two out of the current crop of US presidential candidates are women. Alice Eagly, Christopher Karpowitz, and Lori Beaman, "Why do so few women hold positions of power?" Northwestern University, 2016.

By race, Whites made up the majority of the labor force (79 percent). Blacks and Asians made up an additional 12 percent and 6 percent, respectively. US Bureau of Labor Statistics, Labor force characteristics by race and ethnicity, 2014.

The study on gender diversity by Marcus Noland and colleagues, "Companies with women in leadership roles crush the competition," *Business Insider*, June 17, 2016.

Christopher Cabrera, the chief executive of Xactly, understands the challenge of inherent bias, Adam Bryant, "How to Hire the Right Person," New York Times, 2017.

In one study, researchers found that people used factors in photos like gender and face length to make guesses about people's height and then used these same factors when they judged their leadership qualities. Erin Brodwin, "11 surprising things that your physical appearance says about you," *Business Insider*, August 2, 2016.

Chapter 2

It has been the stage for many movies, like *Good Will Hunting and A Beautiful Mind, MIT* in popular culture. IMDB.

In thinking about partnerships turned into successful ventures coming out of MIT, the story has been told at an annual marketing conference that Brian Halligan and Dharmesh Shah met at MIT Sloan School of Management during their graduate study. HubSpot, About Us.

HubSpot is a marketing platform that's gained a lot of popularity over the years: Ryan Herman, "How to Decide If Your Agency Should Become a HubSpot Partner," 2017.

And building on the teachings of the Hubspotology, personas are fictional, generalized characters: HubSpot Academy, "How to create personas," November 17, 2017.

"The Story Behind Our Story," HubSpot, About Us.

A Leadership Brand conveys your identity and distinctiveness as a leader. It communicates the value you offer: Norm Smallwood, "Define Your Personal Leadership Brand in Five Steps," *Harvard Business Review*, March 29, 2010.

Chapter 4

Organizations often frame the development of leadership concerning "competencies," or the behavioral skills and areas of knowledge required by the business. However, focusing on competencies alone dismisses the critical role that psychological resources play in leadership—especially in today's fast-paced and uncertain global leadership environment: Marian N. Ruderman and Cathleen Clerkin, "Developing Leadership by Building Psychological Capital," Center for Creative Leadership, August 2015.

Chapter 5

The title of one slide is, "The Rare Responsible Person," and the last bullet of that slide is: Picks up trash lying on the floor: Reed Hastings, "The Rare Responsible Person," August 1, 2009.

The best thing leaders can do to improve their effectiveness is to become more aware of what motivates them and their decision-making: Anthony K. Tjan, "How Leaders Become Self-Aware," *Harvard Business Review*, July 19, 2012.

The more you are willing to learn and the harder you are willing to practice, the more successful you will become at achieving your vision and goals. Peter Barron Stark, "6 Skills Even the Strongest Leaders Need to Practice."

Evaluation is the framework for gathering and making sense of information to help you assess the success of leadership development efforts and make sound decisions about future investments. Center for Creative Leadership, "How to Evaluate the Impact of Leadership Development."

Chapter 6

Leaders must be learners: Kelsey Meyer, "Why the Best Leaders Are Full-Time Learners," *Forbes*, June 10, 2013.

Life experiences and our response to them are of critical importance in how leaders are formed and the kind of leaders we become: George Ambler, "How Experiences Shape and Make Leaders," July 29, 2012.

If you are a leader, you should be striving to develop knowledge to improve yourself, your company, and the people who work for you: Kelsey Meyer, "Why Leaders Must Be Readers," *Forbes*, August 3, 2012.

Performance management is the process of identifying, measuring, managing, and developing the performance of the human resources in an organization. Performance appraisal is the ongoing process of evaluating employee performance: Chapter 8: *Performance Management and Appraisal.*

Effective and timely feedback is a critical component of a successful performance management program and should be used in conjunction with setting performance goals. US Office of Personnel Management, "Performance Management."

Chapter 7

Studies prove it: Akhtar, Allana. "11 Scientific Reasons Why Attractive People Are More Successful in Life," *Business Insider*, October 8, 2019.

On average, it takes more than two months before a new behavior becomes automatic—66 days to be exact: James Clear, "How Long Does It Actually Take to Form a New Habit? (Backed by Science)."

The typical chief executive is more than six feet tall, has a deep voice, a good posture, a touch of gray in his thick, lustrous hair, and, for his age, a fit body: "The look of a leader," *The Economist*, September 27, 2014.

Chapter 8

#FridaysForFuture is a movement that began in August 2018, after she and other young activists sat in front of the Swedish parliament every school day for three weeks, to protest against the lack of action on the climate crisis. She posted what she was doing on Twitter and it soon went viral. This was her decision to lead through volunteering. "Fridays For Future Is an International Climate Movement Active in Most Countries and Our Website Offers Information on Who We Are and What You Can Do," *Fridays For Future*.

Chapter 10

Become the kind of leader that people would follow voluntarily, even if you had no title or position. Conduct a personal assessment and ask yourself, "Would I follow me?" Brian Tracy, motivational speaker and author.

Bibliography

Adair, J. E. (2010). *Develop your leadership skills*. Philadelphia: Kogan Page.

Altman, M. W. (2008). *Leadership for all the mountains you climb: while loving the view.* Bloomington, IN: AuthorHouse.

Amabile, T., Schatzel, E., Moneta, G., & Kramer, S. (2004). Leader behaviors and the work environment for creativity: perceived leader support. *The Leadership Quarterly*, 15(1), 5–32.

Antonakis, J., Cianciolo, A. T., & Sternberg, R. J. (2004). *The nature of leadership.* Thousand Oaks, CA: Sage Publications.

Bertocci, D. I. (2009). *Leadership in organizations: there is a difference between leaders and managers.* Lanham, MD: University Press of America.

Bogardus, A. M. (2009). *PHR/SPHR: Professional in Human Resources certification study guide 59* (3rd ed.). Indianapolis, IN: Wiley.

Bolman, L. G. & Deal, T. E. (1997). *Reframing organizations: artistry, choice, and leadership* (5th ed). San Francisco: Jossey-Bass.

Cameron, K. S., & Quinn, R. E. (2011). *Diagnosing and changing organizational culture based on the competing values framework* (3rd ed.). San Francisco: Jossey-Bass.

Cappelli, P. (2011, April 25). Are leaders made or born? www.HREOnline.com.

Carson, M. (2010, September 16). Leadership: is it inherent, can it be taught, or are both true. Free answer: many of the traits that I see with a leader are. www.transtutors .com/questions/tts-leadership-traits-149565.htm.

Chen, W., Jacobs, R., & Spencer, L. M. (1998). *Working with emotional intelligence.* New York: Bantam Books.

Cherry, B., & Jacob, S. R. (2008). *Contemporary nursing: issues, trends & management* (4th ed.). St. Louis, MO: Mosby/ Elsevier.

Cook-Greuter, S. R. (2004, November 7). Industrial and commercial training. industrial and commercial training. www.cook-greuter.com.

Dalakoura, A. (2010). Examining the effects of leadership development on firm ferformance. *Journal of Leadership Studies* 4.1 (2004).

Day, D. V. (n.d.). Developing leadership talent. Society of Human Resources Management.

Deal, T. E., & Kennedy, A. A. (2000). *Corporate cultures: the rites and rituals of corporate life.* Cambridge, MA: Perseus Books.

Drucker, P. F. (1974). *Management: tasks, responsibilities, practices.* New York: Harper & Row.

Dychtwald, K., Erickson, T. J., & Morison, R. (2006). *Workforce crisis: how to beat the coming shortage of skills and talent.* Boston: Harvard Business School Press.

Ennis, S., Goodman, R., Hodgetts, W., Hunt, J., Marshfield, R., & Otto, J. (2005). Core competencies of the executive coach. www.instituteofcoaching.org.

Feldman, H. R. (2005). *Educating nurses for leadership.* New York: Springer.

Folk-Williams, J. (2010, June 4). Defining collaborative leadership. www.crosscollaborate.com.

Frohman, D., & Howard, R. (2008). *Leadership the hard way: why leadership can't be taught and how you can learn it anyway.* San Francisco: Jossey-Bass.

Fulmer, R. M., & Bleak, J. L. (2008). *The leadership advantage: how the best companies are developing their talent to pave the way for future success.* New York: AMACOM/American Management Association.

Gall, M. D., Gall, J. P., & Borg, W. R. (2003). *Educational research: an introduction* (7th ed.). Boston: Allyn and Bacon.

Galton, F. (1869). *Hereditary genius: an inquiry into its laws and consequences.* Cleveland: Meridian Books.

Gardner, H. (1999). *Intelligence reframed: multiple intelligences for the 21st century.* New York: Basic Books.

Garman, A. N., & Harris-Lemak, C. (n.d.). Developing healthcare leaders: what we have learned, and what is next. www.nchl.org.

Giles, Sunnie. (2017, October 25). The most important leadership competencies, according to leaders around the world. *Harvard Business Review.*

Gill, R. (2006). *Theory and practice of leadership.* London: SAGE Publications.

Goleman, Daniel. (1998). *Working with emotional intelligence.* New York: Bantam Books.

Goleman, Daniel, et al. (2016, November 9). The focused leader. *Harvard Business Review.*

Graves, M., & Snyder, N. H. (1994). *Leadership and vision.* Emmitsburg, MD: National Emergency Training Center.

Greeno, N. J. (2006). *Corporate learning strategies.* Alexandria, VA: American Society for Training & Development.

Grenzer, J. W. (2006). *Developing and implementing a corporate university.* Amherst, MA: HRD Press.

Gunderman, R. B. (2009). *Leadership in healthcare.* London: Springer.

Halberstam, D. (2004, September 1). The greatness that cannot be taught | Fast Company | Business + Innovation. *Fast Company.*

Hannum, K., & Martineau, J. W. (2008). *Evaluating the impact of leadership development.* Hoboken, NJ: John Wiley & Sons.

Hannum, K., Martineau, J., & Reinelt, C. (2007). *The handbook of leadership development evaluation.* San Francisco: Jossey-Bass.

Hartley, J., & Benington, J. (2010). *Leadership for healthcare.* Bristol: Policy Press.

Hernez-Broome, G., & Hughes, R. L. (n.d.). Leadership development: past, present, and future. Center for Creative Leadership. www.ccl.org/leadership.

Isaksen, S. G., & Tidd, J. (2006). *Meeting the innovation challenge: leadership for transformation and growth.* Chichester, England: John Wiley.

Jones, B. B., & Brazzel, M. (2006). *The NTL handbook of organization development and change: principles, practices, and perspectives.* San Francisco: Pfeiffer.

Kansal, B. B., & Rao, P. C. K. (2006). *Preface to management.* Daryaganj, New Delhi: Paragon Books.

Kemper, C. L. (1999, October 9). EQ vs. IQ. *Communication World.*

Killian, S. (n.d.). How much should you spend on training?

Kliem, R. L. (2004). *Leading high performance projects.* Boca Raton, FL: J. Ross Pub.

Kouzes, J., & Posner, B. (2003). *The leadership challenge.* San Francisco: Jossey-Bass.

Kretzmann, J. P., & McKnight, J. (1993). *Building communities from the inside out: a path toward finding and mobilizing a community's assets.* Evanston, IL: The Asset-Based Community Development Institute, Institute for Policy Research, Northwestern University.

Latuha, M. (2010). Approaches to corporate training systems for executives: evidence from Russian companies. *Human Resource Development International* 13.2: 207–223.

Lewis, L. K., & Seibold, D. R. (1993). Innovation modification during intraorganizational adoption. *Academy of Management Review* 18.2 (1993) : 332–354.

Malloch, M. (2010). *The SAGE handbook of workplace learning.* Thousand Oaks, CA: SAGE Publications.

Manning, G., & Curtis, K. (2003). *The art of leadership*. Boston: McGraw-Hill/Irwin.

McConnell, J. H. (2003). *How to identify Tour organization's training needs: a practical guide to needs analysis*. New York: AMACOM.

McCrimmon, M. (n.d.). Kouzes and Posner on leadership— a critique. Docstoc.com.

McNally, B. (2000, August 9). Book Review by Beverley McNally of The Leadership Challenge. www.usq.edu.

Modi, T. (2000, June 12). Leadership, whose business is it anyway? teknirvana.com.

Mumford, M. D. (2009). *Leadership 101*. New York: Springer.

Murphy, S. E., & Riggio, R. E. (2003). *The future of leadership development*. Mahwah, NJ: Lawrence Erlbaum Associates.

Ojo, O. (2010). Organisational leadership development for less. *British Journal of Healthcare Management* 73.

Porter-O'Grady, T., & Malloch, K. (2009). *Introduction to evidence-based practice in nursing and health care*. Sudbury, MA: Jones and Bartlett Publishers.

Rothwell, W. J., Lindholm, J. E., & Wallick, W. G. (2003). *What CEOs expect from corporate training building workplace learning and performance initiatives that advance organizational goals.* New York: AMACOM.

Russell, D. B., & Dunne, D. D. (n.d.). How healthy is your company's leadership development culture? *CM eJournal.*

Santana, L. (2008). *Leadership development program: CCL post-program development data.* Greensboro, NC: Center for Creative Leadership.

Sarner, M. (2007, December 19). Can leadership be learned? Fast Company | Business + Innovation. *Fast Company.*

Schein, E. H. (2004). *Organizational culture and leadership.* San Francisco: John Wiley and Sons.

Simonton, D. K. (1994). *Greatness: who makes history and why.* New York: Guilford.

Smallwood, Norm. (2014, July 23). Define your personal leadership brand in five steps. *Harvard Business Review.*

Sostrin, Jesse. (2017, October 23). To be a great leader, you have to learn how to delegate well. *Harvard Business Review.*

Srivastava, S. K. (2005). *Organizational behavior and management.* Darya Gank, New Delhi: Sarup & Sons.

Stowell, C. (2005.). Collaboration: an important leadership development skill.

Ulrich, D., Zenger, J. H., & Smallwood, W. N. (1999). *Results-based leadership*. Boston: Harvard Business School Press.

Weiss, C. H. (1998). *Evaluation: methods for studying programs and policies* (2nd ed.). Upper Saddle River, NJ: Prentice Hall.

Witzel, M. (2005). *The encyclopedia of the history of American management*. Bristol: Thoemmes Continuum.

Young, A. (2010). A structural equation model of leader attributes in the principalship. (Unpublished doctoral dissertation). Clemson University, South Carolina.

About the Author

Catherine M. Rymsha, EdD, knows what makes a leader, a leader. Based on her years of training, research, and consulting, she's determined how a person becomes one: they make the decision to lead.

Catherine is a lecturer at the University of Massachusetts, Lowell, where she teaches courses on leadership. She has taught for Merrimack College and several adult education community programs. Catherine spent over ten years in marketing/communications leadership roles ranging from marketing healthcare conferences to writing speeches on payment card security. She now leads learning and development for a software company. Between her academic and professional experience, she has taught thousands of courses on leadership, feedback, and career to global leaders across an array of industries.

Her TEDx Talk, "Want to Become a Better Leader? Here's How. Just Listen," focuses on the importance of listening to leadership. It can be viewed here: https://www.youtube.com/watch?v=cARuUGgSl7I.

She holds a master of science in leadership and a doctorate of education with a focus on organizational leadership from Northeastern University in Boston and was a member of the Sigma Epsilon Rho honor society. Her research at Northeastern University focuses specifically on leadership development within healthcare.

Catherine received her bachelor of arts in English/communications from the Massachusetts Colleges of Liberal Arts in North Adams, Massachusetts, where she was nominated into "Who's Who Among Students in American Universities and Colleges" and became a member of the Alpha Chi and Lambda Iota Tau honor societies.

Catherine is from West Newbury, Massachusetts, and attended Pentucket Regional High School. She lives on the north shore of Massachusetts with her dog, Mia. She is a four-time marathon runner and an avid snowboarder. Catherine loves craft beer, Nantucket, Massachusetts, and Stowe, Vermont.